T0323709

Cambridge Elements ☰

Elements in Metaphysics
edited by
Tuomas E. Tahko
University of Bristol

PARTS AND WHOLES

Meg Wallace
University of Kentucky

CAMBRIDGE
UNIVERSITY PRESS

Shaftesbury Road, Cambridge CB2 8EA, United Kingdom

One Liberty Plaza, 20th Floor, New York, NY 10006, USA

477 Williamstown Road, Port Melbourne, VIC 3207, Australia

314–321, 3rd Floor, Plot 3, Splendor Forum, Jasola District Centre, New Delhi – 110025, India

103 Penang Road, #05–06/07, Visioncrest Commercial, Singapore 238467

Cambridge University Press is part of Cambridge University Press & Assessment, a department of the University of Cambridge.

We share the University's mission to contribute to society through the pursuit of education, learning and research at the highest international levels of excellence.

www.cambridge.org
Information on this title: www.cambridge.org/9781009087360

DOI: 10.1017/9781009086561

First published 2023

A catalogue record for this publication is available from the British Library.

ISBN 978-1-009-08736-0 Paperback
ISSN 2633-9862 (online)
ISSN 2633-9854 (print)

Parts and Wholes

Elements in Metaphysics

DOI: 10.1017/9781009086561
First published online: May 2023

Meg Wallace
University of Kentucky

Author for correspondence: Meg Wallace

Abstract: The odd universe argument aims to show that from four intuitive assumptions about parts and wholes we can conclude a priori that there is an odd number of things in the universe. This Element investigates how this is so and where things might have gone awry. Section 1 gives an overview of general methodology, basic mereology, and plural logic. Section 2 explores questions about the nature of composition and decomposition. Does composition always occur? Never? Sometimes? Is the universe, at rock bottom, just many partless bits (simples)? Or do the parts have parts all the way down (gunk)? Section 3 looks at arguments for and against the thesis that composition is identity, with a healthy bias in its favor. In the wake of this discussion, we reconsider our methods of counting. We conclude with a return to the odd universe argument and my suggestions on how best to solve it.

Keywords: composition, parts and wholes, mereology, composition as identity, parthood

ISBNs: 9781009087360 (PB), 9781009086561 (OC)
ISSNs: 2633-9862 (online), 2633-9854 (print)

Contents

Introduction: An Odd Universe

Let's start with an implausible claim: *there is an odd number of things in the universe.*[1]

This claim isn't implausible because all evidence suggests otherwise. Or because we have better reason to believe that the total number of things in the universe is *even*. Rather, it's implausible because there doesn't seem to be any reasonable way to defend it.

If we try to prove the claim empirically by counting each thing one by one, it will take too long. All of our lifetimes combined are not enough time to prove that the statement is true. Yet if we try to prove it a priori – by reason alone, *without* going out and taking a look – this seems like mere argumentative magic. How could a priori reasoning yield an answer one way or the other about whether the total number of objects in the universe is even or odd? And why on earth would it be *odd* over even?

Nonetheless, philosophy has a long history of championing a priori arguments for surprising conclusions.[2] Perhaps this would be yet another. Let's give it a shot.

First, some terminology and assumptions. If we want to count up things in the universe, it will help to have an idea of the tiniest bits, the smallest things of which we can go no smaller. These are true atoms, things that cannot be broken down into further parts. A *mereological simple* is an object with no (proper) parts. We will start with the following assumption:

SIMPLES: the universe is, at rock bottom, made up of finitely many mereological simples.

It will also help to know when we have an object and when we do not. Take the chair that you are sitting on. It is an object. But so are the parts of the chair: the legs and the seat. These parts *compose* the chair. So when do some things compose an object and when do they not?[3] Metaphysicians have offered a variety of answers to this question, which we will explore in greater detail in later sections. For now, let us assume the most permissive of answers: *always*. *Unrestricted composition* is the view that *whenever* we have some things, there

---

[1] I was originally introduced to an argument for this claim in Ted Sider's graduate seminar on abstract entities at Syracuse University, fall 2001. It has annoyed me ever since. I present the argument here so that it can now annoy other people, too. Simons (1987: 17) mentions a similar argument, but doesn't discuss it in detail. A version appears in Roy Sorenson (2003: 360–362), where he attributes it to John Robinson, in response to Nelson Goodman's (1951) *The Structure of Appearances*. It is also mentioned in Wallace (2014a).

[2] For example, the ontological argument for the existence of god, Descartes' *cogito*, Lewis' arguments for a plurality of possible worlds.

[3] This is a version of Peter van Inwagen's Special Composition Question (SCQ), discussed in Section 2.

is a composite object – a mereological sum – composed of those things. This is our second assumption.

UNRESTRICTED COMPOSITION: for any things whatsoever, there is an object composed of these things.

It is worth pausing to reflect for a moment on the extraordinary implications of this view. The handle of your coffee mug is a thing. The right paw of my cat Zuki is a thing. According to unrestricted composition, there is a mereological sum – an object – composed of the handle of your coffee mug and Zuki's right paw. This object is distinct from the mereological sum of the top half of your coffee mug and Zuki's tail, which is also an object. Composite objects are *everywhere*, even if many of these objects are not ones we usually consider or care about.

It will also help to think about the *relation* between the parts of an object and the whole that those parts compose. Take your chair again, and the parts that compose it. Are these parts *distinct* from the chair? It certainly seems so. There is only one chair, yet there are many parts. We can take the chair apart so that *it* no longer exists, but the parts still do. The parts can be scattered across the room but the chair cannot. The parts existed before the chair, yet the chair might exist after the parts disappear. The chair can survive a replacement of its parts, but the parts cannot survive a replacement of themselves. And so on. While these considerations may not help us figure out what the composition relation *is*, it does help determine what it is *not*: composition is *not* identity.

COMPOSITION IS NOT IDENTITY: the relation between parts and wholes – composition – is *not* the identity relation.

Finally, if we want to count the things in the universe, we have to *count*. Let's start with the things on my desk. I look around and itemize each thing individually. "Here's a coffee mug, there's another coffee mug, here's a water bottle, there's a keyboard, there's a lazy cat, there's Zuki." I then consider whether any of the things listed are identical or not. "The coffee mug over here is not identical to the coffee mug over there, so there are at least two things. Neither of the two coffee mugs are identical to the water bottle, the keyboard, or the lazy cat, so that's at least five things. The lazy cat just *is* Zuki; she is just one thing, included in the five things I just listed. So, there are still five things." Intuitively, this is all it takes to take a count: we tally up all of the things that we think that there are, together with the relevant identity (and nonidentity) claims that are true of these things.

COUNT: we count by listing what there is together with the relevant identity (and nonidentity) claims.

Next, the argument. Suppose there is a world with only one mereological simple, *a*. How many objects are in this world? Intuitively, just one: *a*. Assuming *unrestricted composition*, we also have the mereological sum of *a*. Yet the mereological sum of one thing just *is* that one thing; the mereological sum of *a* is *identical to a*.[4] So, given *count*, there is one thing in this world – an odd number.

Suppose we add another simple, *b*. Now how many objects are in this world? Intuitively, two: *a* and *b*. Yet if we assume unrestricted composition, then in addition to the mereological sum of each simple to itself (which is just each simple, *a*, *b*), there is *also* the sum of *a and b*, *ab*. Assuming that *composition is not identity*, *ab* is not identical to *a*, nor is it identical to *b*. So, there are three things in this world: *ab*, *a*, and *b* – an odd number.

If we add another mereological simple to our world, *c*, the same sort of reasoning applies. We have the simples, *a*, *b*, and *c*. But we also have all of the mereological sums that result from unrestricted composition: *ab*, *bc*, *ac*, and *abc*, none of which are identical to the parts that compose them. So, there are seven things in the world – an odd number. *Keep going.*

However many simples we start with, *n*, unrestricted composition entails that we also have all of the mereological sums of those simples (and mereological sums of any mereological sums). Because we are assuming that composition is *not* identity, none of these additional sums will be identical to any of the parts that compose them. Assuming *count*, we can calculate the number of things in any world, starting with *n* simples, as $2^n - 1$.[5] This will always be an odd number. So, there is an odd number of things in the universe.

Call this the *odd universe argument*. Is this argumentative magic? Or a legitimate a priori proof of an odd universe?

Maybe you do not find yourself gripped by the problem. After all, the universe is a pretty big place. Perhaps it's so big that we don't have strong opinions about how many things are in it one way or the other. Yet keep in mind: the problem is not just the implausibility of the conclusion. Rather, it's because we don't expect that an a priori argument will deliver a verdict on such matters. Focusing on the number of things in the entire universe is certainly dramatic, but ultimately unnecessary; the odd universe argument can be repurposed to fit any domain. We can just as easily conclude that there is an odd number of things in Kentucky. Or in your room. On your desk. In the sock drawer. The reasoning is fully generalizable – and thus unacceptable. Unless we accept that there is an odd number of things any place we look, one of the assumptions must go.

---

[4] This follows from principles of classical extensional mereology, a formal theory of parts and wholes discussed in Section 1.2.

[5] We'll go over why we subtract 1 in Section 1.2.2.

Perhaps *unrestricted composition* should be rejected. We've already seen some of the extraordinary consequences of thinking that mereological sums abound. But what are the alternatives? Should we think that there are *no* composite sums, as the mereological nihilist does? Or that there are some composite sums, but not others, as the mereological moderate does? Yet how do we stake out a moderate view without being arbitrary, anthropocentric, or ad hoc?

Perhaps we shouldn't assume that the universe is constituted by finitely many partless bits. Or perhaps there is something incoherent in the notion of a partless bit, no matter how many. But what are the alternatives? Should we assume instead that there are *infinitely* many simples? Can we know a priori that the universe has infinitely many things? If this sounds implausible, maybe we should reject the idea of simples, *tout court*. Perhaps there are parts *all the way down*, with no 'rock bottom.' But this seems to imply that even just where my coffee mug sits, there are infinitely many things! This also seems to vindicate Zeno-type worries: we'll have trouble moving across the room because there are infinitely many parts to traverse to get there.

Perhaps we should rethink the nature of the composition relation. Perhaps composition is, in fact, *identity*. But what about the reasons we stated above? The parts have features that the whole does not, and the whole has features that the parts do not. Isn't this enough to show that parts are *not* identical to wholes, even if they compose them?

Maybe we made a mistake in thinking we know how to count. We assumed that by quantifying over all of the things that there are, together with any relevant identity or nonidentity statements, that this yields an answer as to how many objects there are. Should we be counting differently? Should we, as Frege and others have suggested, count by concepts or kinds? Is it incoherent to think that we can take an inventory of *things, simpliciter*? Or do we have to have a certain concept or kind in mind before taking a count makes sense?

What follows is an exploration into some of these options, as well as some others. The result will be an opinionated overview of some of the main metaphysical issues involving parts and wholes, guided by a diagnosis of why we *shouldn't* conclude a priori that there are an odd number of things in the universe. Many of the sections are stand-alone, even if they are related or refer to others. My hope is that readers can easily skip around to topics that interest them without having to invest in the main thread. This is also written for those unfamiliar with the literature. Those looking for a more advanced or in-depth analysis of specialized topics will be referred to relevant resources along the way.

Here's what to expect. Section 1 gives a brief overview of general methodology, basic mereology, and plural logic. Section 2 explores questions about the nature of composition and decomposition. Does composition always occur? Never? Sometimes? Is the universe, at rock bottom, just many partless bits (simples)? Or do the parts have parts all the way down (gunk)? Section 3 looks at arguments in support of (and against) the thesis that composition is identity, with a healthy bias in its favor. In the wake of this discussion, we reconsider our methods of counting. We conclude with some reflections on how best to maneuver around the odd universe.

1 Parts and Plurals

Let's begin by recognizing how we *in fact* talk about parts and wholes away from the philosophy room.[6]

1. My elbow is part of my arm.
2. My arm is part of my body.
3. Because of 1 and 2, my elbow is part of my body.
4. Those stars compose the constellation.
5. These two roads overlap at the intersection.
6. The Statue of Liberty and my left big toe have no part in common.
7. The first act is the most boring part of the play.
8. This is the complicated part of the argument.
9. She is part of the rebel alliance.
10. The larval stage is part of a bug's life.
11. That was a dark part of history.
12. Trigonometry is part of mathematics.
13. Omniscience is part of God's nature.
14. "Don't eat animals" is part of his moral code.
15. Her donation is part of what made his project possible.
16. That she could do it is part of the reason she did.

Sentences 1 and 2 refer to bodily parts, things that are spatially extended. Sentence 3 captures our intuition that the parthood relation is *transitive*: if x is part of y and y is part of z, then x is part of z. Sentence 4 indicates that *compose* is a many–one relation: 'those stars' is plural, 'the constellation' is singular. Sentence 5 is evidence that we take the concept of *overlap* – sharing a part – to be unproblematic and intuitive, while 6 indicates that we understand what it is for things to be *disjoint* – to have *no* parts in common.

---

[6] Sentences 7 and 10 are adapted from Simons (1987: 22), 12 and 13 from Lewis (1991: 75).

Sentences 7–16 indicate that we use parts–whole concepts to apply to a wide range of entities: narratives, groups/organizations/movements, arguments, events, topics/subjects, properties, actions, explanations, norms, possibilities, and reasons. Depending on our particular metaphysical views of these things, this may imply that in addition to spatially extended, concrete material objects such as bodies, stars, roads, and statues, we apply our parts–whole concepts to immaterial or abstract things (7, 8, 11, 12, 14), concrete–abstract or material–immaterial hybrids (9, 10, 13, 15), increments of time (10, 11), and possibilities or possible worlds (14, 15, 16). Parts can be attached and unscattered (1–3) or unattached and scattered (4), homogeneous (1, 2, 3, 12) or heterogeneous (4, 8, 10, 13, 15, 16), and so on. (We will often be referring back to these sentences, so let's keep them in mind in the pages that follow.)

1.1 Methodology

Appealing to our ordinary uses of parts–whole terminology to initiate more formal theorizing about such things is a common strategy in the literature on parts and wholes.[7] In *Parts of Classes*, for example, David Lewis justifies many of the principles of the formal study of parts and wholes (mereology) by appealing to what we ordinarily think and say. There's an assumption that our parts–whole concepts involve some of our most fundamental intuitions about the world.

Yet it is certainly possible to question the effectiveness of this approach. Perhaps common opinion about parts and wholes doesn't track the underlying reality of how the world really works. Ordinary intuitions about *metaphysics* may be as (un)reliable as ordinary intuitions about *physics*. Ordinary folk have thought (and sometimes still do think) that the world is flat, that distinct solid objects can be in contact with one another and are *not* mostly empty space, that the world is guided by causal determinism or Newtonian laws of nature, and so on. Very rarely does this bother the physicist. She does not halt or alter her research because it runs contrary to ordinary opinion. So perhaps the metaphysician should likewise be unbothered by common sense – in which case we metaphysicians should stop appealing to what we ordinarily think and say.

Of course, this isn't quite right. The scientist *does* in fact have to be accountable to our everyday experiences, even if her theory seems to differ wildly from them. Endorsing a theory about why solid objects are mostly empty space still requires an explanation as to why it seems to us as if they aren't. Defending

---

[7] See, e.g., Simons (1987), Sider (2007), McDaniel (2010a), Varzi (2019), and Cotnoir and Varzi (2021).

a view of the solar system where the earth is not the center still requires providing an explanation for why it nonetheless seems to us as if it is. Similarly, any philosopher promoting a view that is grossly counterintuitive is under pressure to provide an explanation for our mistaken impressions, or else she will need to somehow minimize her view so that the impact to common sense isn't so jarring.[8]

It may help to keep in mind what (some) metaphysicians take themselves to be doing when thinking philosophically about the underlying nature of reality. We're often trying to systematically explore our most fundamental notions. We're trying to take how we in fact think about the world and regiment it, so that it is principled and coherent. If our usage is contradictory or confused, then this provides some reason to reconsider or refine our usage; yet if our theorizing is too far removed from how we in fact *use* our ordinary concepts, this provides some reason to think that our theorizing is substantially off-topic. Simons (1987: 106) puts the point this way:

> Clearly a formal theory cannot adhere slavishly to usage if this usage is conflicting and/or if its formalization would result in an inconsistent theory. Against that, a formal theory claiming to represent – even in part – or regiment a concept in general use, such as that of 'part', cannot lose all sight of the informal usage from which it is intended to derive its interpretation and plausibility. A compromise between these two unacceptable extremes has to be found, but it is no easy matter to determine where.

This suggests a strategy of *cautious equilibrium*. We can use common sense to motivate various philosophical positions about parts and wholes, as a fallible guide or defeasible check against our philosophical theories: *fallible* and *defeasible* because sometimes the fact that a view is contrary to common sense is a mark against the theory, but sometimes the rigor and plausibility of the theory is a mark against common sense. In lieu of principled criteria to determine when to do what, we'll proceed on a case by case basis in what follows, and hope, in the end, for a sensible balance between theory and use (see Lycan 2019).

1.2 Mereology

The things in my pocket were put there by my four year old: a scraggly bird feather, a small blue rock, a piece of string. Until I mentioned them, we had no need to think of these things as part of a group or collection. They don't, under

---

[8] I have in mind here what Karen Bennett (2009) calls "difference-minimizing." See, e.g., van Inwagen (1990: 98–114). Not all philosophers feel compelled to difference-minimize – e.g., Unger (1979a, 1979b).

ordinary circumstances, seem to be three parts of a cohesive whole. Yet once they are in my pocket, and I understand them to be part of the collection of trinkets that my toddler collected this morning, they then become (or are recognized to be or can be thought of as) parts of a whole. It is quite striking that we are able to do this with any random things at all, at any time we please.

It is also quite striking that we can do this even when the things under consideration are not material, are not clearly conceivable, or are indeterminate or infinite in number. Consider all of the blue things that exist, everywhere, and think of the group that has only these things as parts. This is the collection of *existing blue things*. Maybe we can't clearly picture them in our head or produce an accurate guess of their number, like we would if we were to imagine the collection of *blue things in my room*. But we certainly understand the conditions under which some things would be part of the group *existing blue things* and which things would not. Likewise, consider the collection of *anything that ever was, is, or will be blue*. Or *things that are possibly blue*. Neither of these collections are easily imaginable, nor would they be finite in number, but the description is certainly coherent: we understand what it takes for something to be part of this whole, and what it takes for something to *not* be part of it.

The second part of this last point is noteworthy. Just as we have the ability to think of some things composing a whole, we also have the ability to think of some things that are *not* part of a whole, to think of things sectioned off from other things, distinct from a unity. We can also think about how a unity breaks down into other things, via *decomposition*. Given that we so easily think and talk about many things as one, as parts to wholes, then perhaps such unities of things *exist*.

Our ability to think in these ways about parts and wholes is similar to our ability to think through novel sentences in a language or to think through unfamiliar inferences in logic. Logic is the formal study of what follows from what. It is a system that aims to match our ordinary intuitions about which inferences are ok and which are not. Beginning with just some basic terms and functions, we can generate or understand any arguments we please, even entirely new ones. In language, once we have a basic stock of vocabulary and rules, we can then generate any sentences we please, even ones that have never been uttered or thought of before. That we can do this is (arguably) some evidence that the basic elements – the formal structures – can be captured and regimented. One of the aims of formal language and logic is to systematize this structure that governs our actual *use* of linguistic and logical concepts. Likewise, one of the aims of *mereology* is to systematize the structure that governs our actual use of parts–whole concepts.

The analogy between language, logic, and mereology is admittedly imperfect, but nonetheless helpful. There are many (infinitely many) sentences in language and arguments in logic that are technically well-formed, yet only a small subset of these are ones that we use or care about. This doesn't make the unused or uncared-for sentences any less well-formed, or any less instructive for the purposes of learning language or logic. Likewise, we may think that mereology gives us the tools to think of a wide range of objects (wholes), even if only a small subset of these are ones we in fact use or care about.

A quick clarification. Some consider mereology to be a broad topic of inquiry that covers any kind of theorizing about parts and wholes. Interpreted this way, philosophers have been thinking about mereology since at least as early as Parmenides, who entertained the idea of the world as a unified, undivided whole, or Zeno who argued that, on pain of paradox, there could be neither infinitely nor finitely many parts, and, thus, there are no parts whatsoever.[9] Others reserve the term 'mereology' to refer to the systematic study of parts and wholes, involving a formal language, such as the one introduced by Stanislaw Leśniewski (1927–31), developed by Leonard and Goodman (1940), and discussed in Simons (1987).[10] This second interpretation is our focus in what follows.

A quick note. I aim to keep Section 1.2.1 informal and in plain language as much as possible, even though I'll be walking through a formal system; all formal terminology will be explained informally. For anyone who would rather not bother, skim ahead to 1.2.2 or 1.2.3. The following is intended to provide some useful – but optional – background.

1.2.1 Axioms and Definitions

We'll begin by taking 'part' as primitive. We'll then define other mereological concepts in terms of this concept.[11]

Let "$x \leq y$" represent "x is part of y":

Reflexivity: $\forall x \; x \leq x$

Antisymmetry: $\forall x \forall y \; ((x \leq y \; \& \; y \leq x) \rightarrow x = y)$

Transitivity: $\forall x \forall y \forall z \; ((x \leq y \; \& \; y \leq z) \rightarrow x \leq z)$

Reflexivity is the claim that everything is part of itself. This may sound counterintuitive. We do not often say things like "my arm is part of my arm" or "this

---

[9] See Harte (2002) for a discussion of Plato's views on parts and wholes. See, e.g., Salmon (2001), Sainsbury (2009), and Huggett (2019) on Zeno's paradox.

[10] For excellent overviews, see Lando (2017), Varzi (2019), and Cotnoir and Varzi (2021).

[11] Taking 'part' as primitive is not our only option. Simons (1987) uses 'proper part'; Leonard and Goodman (1940) use 'discreteness' (or: disjointness); Goodman (1951) uses 'overlaps.' Nearly all agree that whichever primitive is chosen, the other relevant notions can be defined in terms of it; although, see Kleinschmidt (2019). See also Hovda (2009), Parsons (2014).

brick is part of itself." Instead, we say things like "my elbow is part of my arm" (sentence 1) or "my arm is part of my body" (sentence 2). We typically think of *parts* as something smaller or less than or a subsection of whatever the parts are *parts of*. Being a part of some whole *seems* to imply that there is a remainder – whatever is left after the part is removed.

Yet imagine a wall with a small brick part, 'Brick.' We can imagine Brick getting bigger and bigger, until the one (big!) Brick composes the whole wall. Consider the moment right before Brick composes the whole wall. Perhaps there's one small bit – a tiny speck, 'Speck' – of the wall that is not Brick. We can grant that Brick is the biggest part, and takes up almost the whole wall, along with Speck, who is barely noticeable, as small as a grain of sand. Still, Brick is part of the wall, as is Speck. Now imagine that Speck blows away, and all that's left is Brick. Intuitively, Brick is still part of the wall; Brick *is* the wall! Nothing has happened to Brick at all. It is Speck that has blown away. This example may help to massage our intuitions in favor of *reflexivity*, and to understand how identity is the limiting case of parthood (see Armstrong 1978: 37).

Antisymmetry is the claim that anything(s) that are parts of each other are identical. Another way to put it: distinct things cannot be parts of each other. Contrast this with symmetrical relations such as *next to* and *concurrent with*: if Al is next to Bob, Bob is next to Al; if the rainstorm is concurrent with the baseball game, the baseball game is concurrent with the rainstorm. The *part of* relation is not like this: if my arm is part of my body – given that my arm is *not* my body – my body is *not* part of my arm. Antisymmetry captures the intuition that proper parthood is *not* symmetric, while also being consistent with the limiting case of identity, which is.

Transitivity is the claim that the parthood relation is transitive: if my elbow is part of my arm, and my arm is part of my body, then my elbow is part of my body (sentence 3).

Any relation that is reflexive, antisymmetric, and transitive is, by definition, a partial ordering. So *parthood* is a partial order.

Some may consider the above axioms as mere stipulations of an artificial formal system. Others see them as an articulation of the basic structure of what our parts–whole concepts *are*. Peter Simons claims, "These principles are partly constitutive of the meaning of 'part', which means that anyone who seriously disagrees with them has failed to understand the word" (1987: 11). Going back to our discussion of methodology a moment ago, we will proceed under the assumption that the notion of 'part' that mereology aims to capture is the same as that in use in our everyday talk (such as sentences 1–16). This includes those concepts that we employ when we think of parts, generally, such as any random things as part of a unified whole, as parts sectioned off from a whole, or as a whole divided into parts.

Using the above axioms, we can define other mereological relations, such as *proper parthood, overlap,* and *disjointness*.

Proper Parthood (PP): $x < y =_{df} x \leq y \ \& \ x \neq y$

Overlap: $xOy =_{df} \exists z(z \leq x \ \& \ z \leq y)$

Disjointness: $xDy =_{df} \neg xOy$

Proper parthood captures our intuition that certain parts are less than or nonidentical to wholes. Any unintuitiveness we might have felt about the reflexivity axiom can be assuaged by using the distinction between *parthood* (or *improper parthood*), which allows a thing to be part of itself, and *proper parthood*, which does not. One might plausibly claim that our ordinary part–whole utterances (such as sentences 1–16) pick out proper parthood, which can then be defined in terms of an improper parthood relation.

Overlap expresses the idea that one thing overlaps another just in case they have a part in common. Lots of ordinary objects we encounter every day appear to overlap by sharing a part. Roads overlap by sharing the intersection (sentence 5), rooms overlap by sharing a wall, academic courses overlap by sharing content, and so on. Generally, the concept of overlap is assumed to be intuitive and unmysterious.

Disjointness is the opposite of overlap. If two objects are disjoint, then they have no part in common. The moon and your ham sandwich, the Statue of Liberty and my left big toe (sentence 6), triangularity and circularity are all disjoint because they lack any shared parts. They have no section of overlap.

Given these axioms and definitions, we can then introduce further claims about how and under what conditions some things compose a whole. First, we need a way of picking out some objects *plurally*, not just singularly. Consider a sentence such as "the students surrounded the building." We do not typically mean by this sentence that there is a single thing that surrounded the building. Rather, we mean that many things – the students *together* – surrounded the building. This is a collective use of 'the students.' Contrast this with "the students aced the exam," where we intend that each student, individually, aced the exam. This is a distributive use of 'the students.' To capture this difference, let's use capital variables such as "X" to refer to "the *x*s" *collectively*, not *distributively*.

We also need an *inclusion* predicate – a way of expressing that some object is among some other objects. An expression such as "$z \preccurlyeq X$" will mean that "z is one of the X." We then define a *fusion* (or sum) as follows.

Fusion (sum): $yFX =_{df} \forall w(wOy \leftrightarrow \exists z(z \preccurlyeq X \ \& \ wOz))$[12]

This says: y is a fusion of some things, X, when y overlaps exactly those things that overlap something that is one of the X. That is, when something y overlaps all and only those things that overlap whatever is one of the X, y is the fusion of the X.

It is worth noting that the definition of 'fusion' employed here does not assume anything about what *kind* of thing the fused thing is – it is highly general. So, for example, the fusion of all cats is not assumed to be a cat, the fusion of some molecules is not assumed to be a molecule, the fusion of ideas is not one big idea. Nor is any fusion of anything assumed to be some abstract entity like a set or number. It is not a metaphysical lasso or container. A fusion is simply a whole – a collection or a group – whose only conditions for existence are that it has certain things as parts.

Once we have a definition of 'fusion,' we can further specify characteristics of fusions with *unrestricted fusion* and *uniqueness*.[13]

Unrestricted Fusion: $\forall Y \exists x(xFY)$

Uniqueness: $(xFY \ \& \ zFY) \rightarrow x = z$

Unrestricted fusion is the mereological principle behind one of our assumptions in the odd universe argument, *unrestricted composition*.[14] It claims that *whenever* there are some things, there is a fusion of those things. This (arguably) captures our ability to think of *any* random things at all, together as a whole, collection, or group. For *any* things at all – whatever things you like – there is a fusion of those things that we can think about, talk about, name, quantify over, and so on.

Uniqueness captures the idea that any fusion of all and only some parts will be the only fusion of those parts. That is, if some x fuses the Ys and some z fuses the Ys, x is identical to z. Since there is nothing else to being a whole aside from having certain things as parts, then anything that has those same parts is the same whole.

In addition to thinking about how things might compose, we might also think about how things decompose.

---

[12] Different mereological systems propose different definitions of 'fusion.' I follow Goodman (1951) here, somewhat modified, as well as Simons (1987) and Casati and Varzi (1999). See Hovda (2009) and Cotnoir and Varzi (2021). I use 'fusion' and 'sum' interchangeably.

[13] These claims are a bit more controversial and worth thinking through. For further reading, see Cotnoir and Varzi (2021).

[14] For expository purposes, I've introduced 'unrestricted *fusion*' and 'unrestricted *composition*' separately to acknowledge that the former is an axiom of formal mereology, whereas the latter is not; more discussion follows in Section 2.1.

Supplementation: $\forall x \forall y (x < y \rightarrow \exists z\, (z \leq y \land zDx))$

Supplementation captures the idea that a proper part leaves a *remainder* – another proper part. Any proper part is *supplemented* by another proper part(s), which together compose the relevant whole. If x is a proper part of y, then some part of y – namely, z – is disjoint from x.

The above formulation is *weak supplementation*, in contrast with *strong supplementation*, which says that in the case where x is not part of y, then some part of x – namely, z – is disjoint from y: $(\forall x \forall y (x \not\leq y \rightarrow \exists z\, (z \leq x\; \&\; zDy)))$. There is some debate about which formulation most accurately captures our intuitions, and these decisions have ramifications for our views on decomposition and extensionality. We won't go into these issues here; see Simons (1987), Hovda (2009), and Cotnoir and Varzi (2021) for discussion.

1.2.2 Sets and Sums

Mereology is just one way philosophers (and others) have tried to capture our ability to systematically think about many things collected together as one. Another is set theory.[15] It is no surprise, then, that Leonard and Goodman (1940: 45) begin their seminal paper with a comparison of mereological sums (individuals) with sets (classes): "The concept of an individual and that of a class may be regarded as different devices for distinguishing one segment of the total universe from all that remains. In both cases, the differentiated segment is potentially divisible, and may even be physically discontinuous."

Sets are collections of things that are completely characterized by the things that are collected. The things collected are the members (or elements), which are members of a set (the collection). Set theory contains a number of axioms and definitions, although set theory arguably came first (cf. Cotnoir and Varzi (2021:4–5)). Mereology was introduced as an *alternative* to set theory in order to avoid Russell's paradox and to provide a nominalist-friendly foundation for mathematics – i.e., a system that would be less ontologically burdensome.[16]

Because sets and mereological fusions (sums) are both systematic attempts to capture our intuitions about how it is that many things can be collected together as one, there are many similarities between them. Yet there are some important differences. A collection defined by its members can intuitively come apart from a collection defined by its parts. The *set* of the northern hemisphere and the southern hemisphere is distinct from the set of the eastern hemisphere and the

---

[15] For two excellent overviews, see Bagaria (2021) and Burgess (2022).

[16] Leśniewski (1927–31) introduces mereology as a way to avoid Russell's paradox, as well as to have a nominalistic alternative to set theory. Goodman (1951, 1977) primarily uses it for this latter reason. More on both of these later in this section.

western hemisphere. Different members, different sets. However, the mereo-logical *sum* of the northern hemisphere and southern hemisphere is identical to the sum of the eastern and western hemisphere. Since every geographical and physical part of the northern and southern hemispheres exactly overlaps every geographical and physical part of the eastern and western hemispheres, they are the same mereological sum or fusion. Different parts do not entail different sums.

Sets and sums fall under different ontological categories. Sets are abstract, whereas sums (arguably) inherit their metaphysical makeup from their parts. The set of you and me is not identical to you and me: it is not located where we are, it existed before we did, and will exist after we are gone. It is an abstract entity even if the members are not. The mereological sum of you and me, in contrast, is concrete, because the relevant parts (you and me) are concrete. The sum of the color blue and triangularity, on the other hand, is abstract, because the parts are. Meanwhile, the sum of the northern hemisphere and the color blue is arguably concrete *and* abstract, since one part is concrete and one part is abstract, whereas the set of such things is abstract.

Set theory and mereology also differ as to whether there is something that is *null*: a set with no member, or a sum with no parts. According to set theory, there is a null set (the empty set), but according to mereology, there is no null individual (partless sum).[17] Every set has the empty set as a subset, but the empty set itself has no members. In contrast, there is no individual without parts in mereology. There is no fusion of nothing. It is compatible with mereology that there are individuals without *proper* parts – mereological simples. But mereology itself doesn't tell us whether there *are* such things or not. It merely provides us with a theoretical framework wherein having such things is permis-sible. There are sets with one member, called *singletons*. Yet a singleton set is distinct from the one member of that singleton set – e.g., the singleton of Socrates is distinct from Socrates.

In contrast, an object with only one part just *is* the object itself – e.g., the sum of a mereological simple is identical to that simple. Connecting back up to the odd universe argument for a minute, this is why in a world with just one mereological simple, there is only one object. Moreover, because – according to classical extensional mereology – there is no null individual, we subtract 1 when counting up sums - i.e., our formula for figuring out how many objects there are in the odd universe argument is 2^n-1. Any calculation of the number of individuals will need to discount the null individual.

---

[17] According to some mereological systems, the prohibition of a null individual is listed as an axiom; in others, it is derived or entailed by other axioms.

Statements about sets and sums have different logical consequences or entailments. In particular, naive classical extensional set theory gives rise to paradox but classical extensional mereology does not. One of the reasons Leśniewski gives for preferring mereological sums over sets is to avoid Russell's paradox, which arises when we consider the set of all sets which are not members of themselves (Simons 1987: 102). In naive set theory, not every set is a member of itself, so for the set of all sets that do not have themselves as members, does it have itself as a member or not? If it does, then it doesn't; if it doesn't, then it does. Either way lies a contradiction – a devastating consequence for set theory. In mereology, as we have seen, everything is a part of itself. So there is no mereological equivalent to Russell's paradox. There is no mereological sum of all sums that are not part of themselves, because *everything* is part of itself.

Some claim that certain consequences follow from these differences – for example, that no set is ever a sum. Lewis (1991) notably resists this inference; his *Parts of Classes* is an exploration into how mereological sums apply to sets (classes), as well as other things. Whether Lewis is correct or whether mereology and set theory should remain distinct ways of thinking about the structure of reality are not issues I will explore here. My purpose in delineating some of the differences between sets and sums is merely to help clarify what a mereological sum *is*.

1.2.3 Ontological Innocence

In addition to not landing us in paradox as set theory does, mereological sums can be presumed to have other advantages over sets. One is that mereological sums are often advertised as being *ontologically innocent*, whereas sets are not. A commitment to the mereological sum of a and b, ab, is not supposed to be *something over and above* a commitment to a and a commitment to b. Of course, just what exactly 'ontological innocence' is, or what it means for something not to be 'over and above' some other things, are controversial matters.

One way to interpret 'ontological innocence' is *quantitatively*. If mereological sums are quantitatively ontologically innocent, then if we already have a and we already have b, we do not have something additional – we do not literally add to the number of entities that there are – when we have the mereological sum ab.

There are a couple of related assumptions in the background here. One is a Quinean criterion of ontological commitment. Quine (1948) claims that we are ontologically committed to those things that our best theory of the world says that there are. If our best overall theory of the world existentially quantifies over tables and chairs, then there are tables and chairs. If it says that there are numbers, then there are numbers. If mereology becomes part of our best overall theory of the world, then we need to take a look at what mereology says that there is, by looking at the kinds of entities that it existentially quantifies over. Yet aside from the conditional claim about when there are fusions – *always*, whenever we have some things – mereology doesn't say whether there are any things to begin with, how many, or what kinds of things they are. Mereology is one thing, ontology is another.

Suppose we come to mereology already committed to a bunch of things – coffee mugs, running shoes, the color blue. Once we have these things, does the adoption of mereology give us anything else? Do mereological sums give us *quantitatively more* items in our domain than we had prior to admission of those sums?

Consider for comparison an example from Lewis (1994). Imagine a dot matrix image composed of a million tiny pixels. Each pixel can be either light or dark, and as the dots change, so too does the overall image. We do not have a change in the image without a change in the dots that comprise it. The resulting image is "nothing over and above the pixels"; it "could go unmentioned in an inventory of what there is without thereby rendering the inventory incomplete" (1994: 53). Lewis uses this particular example to motivate his discussion about supervenience and reduction as they apply to mental events. But in so doing, he suggests a general diagnostic for determining ontological innocence (or guilt) of any entity in our ontology. We imagine that we are taking an inventory or tally of all the things in the world. We *count up* all the things that we think there are, and then we see whether the suspicious entity is an additional thing. If we've counted each individual dot in a dot matrix picture, do we count the resulting image, too? Or would that be double counting?

How do we know whether we've double counted something or not? Think back to one of our suppositions in the odd universe argument: *count*. To count things up, we take the existential claims we think are true (via our Quinean criterion of ontological commitment), together with the identity and nonidentity claims we accept. Intuitively, we have *double counted a* and *b* if we quantify over *a* and *b* separately, yet *a* is identical to *b*. When tallying up all the things in my room, if I list *the lazy cat* and *Zuki* separately, even though the lazy cat just is Zuki, then I have mistakenly counted the cat twice.

Double counting is not just a way of getting counts *wrong*, however. It can also be a way of determining whether something is ontologically innocent. An entity is ontologically innocent if adding it to our inventory of existing things results in double counting. So, for example, mereological sums will be ontologically innocent if adding them to our inventory of existing things (the parts) results in counting things twice.

One way to do this: suppose that mereological sums are *identical* to the parts that compose them – that is, assume that composition is identity. Since, on pain of double counting, we cannot count mereological sums as distinct from the parts, sums are ontologically innocent. Other ways to do this are to assume that mereological sums are supervenient upon, or reducible to, or somehow or another already included in all of the stuff that we have prior to adoption of sums.[18] Some may argue that given the definition of *fusion* in mereology, ontological innocence is already implied. According to this definition, the only conditions for existence of a fusion is there being a thing that overlaps (shares parts with) some other things. Since our notion of 'part' is highly general, and since all that is needed is the existence of the whole that overlaps some parts, which is also highly general, we might think that this is how mereological sums come along for 'free.'

A second way to interpret 'ontological innocence' is *qualitatively* (cf. Lewis 1973: 87). If mereological sums are qualitatively ontologically innocent, then if we already have *a* and *b*, we do not have a *new kind of thing* when we get the mereological sum of *a* and *b*, *ab*.[19] To contrast with sets again, sets are often considered something over and above the members, primarily because of the *kind* of thing that sets are. Sets are abstract whereas the members may not be. Are mereological sums a new kind of thing from the parts that compose them, in the way that sets are? Or in the way that (some argue) mental entities are different in kind from the physical entities that give rise to them? Or are they more like a dot matrix image, where the overall image is not different in kind from the dots that constitute the image?

If we mean by 'mereological sums' the highly generalized notion we seem to use when thinking of any random things as part of a whole, this doesn't seem to entail the existence of something different in *kind* in the way that a commitment to mental events might. In tandem with our assumption about Quinean criteria of ontological commitments is the idea that to be or to exist – to be a thing in our ontology – is "to be the value of a variable." That's it. The 'thing' in question does not have to be material, concrete, extended spatially or temporally, or contemplated in the mind of god. *To be something that exists* is understood in the widest possible sense: it is whatever it is that is quantified over by our best overall theory of the world. There are no restrictions about what kind of things the existing things have to be. This view, coupled with the core axioms and

---

[18] I don't have the space to explore these options here, but the literature on composition as identity is a great place to start. See below (Section 3) for further discussion and references.

[19] Issues about *how* qualitative and quantitative costs are related, while interesting and important, will not be addressed here.

definitions of mereology, may imply that mereological sums are not qualitatively extra kinds of things.

Finally, a third way mereology is presumed to be ontologically innocent is that, aside from the mereological facts and relations, it doesn't make any assumptions about what the world has to be like, or what kinds of things have to be in it in order for the mereological facts and relations to hold. Questions about parts and wholes and how they are related (composition) are separable from ontological questions about what sorts of things are in the world. We should be able to coherently imagine lots of different ways the metaphysical makeup of the world could be while still obeying the rules of mereology. A Berkelean idealist, who thinks that all there is are immaterial minds and ideas, can still think about whether this immaterial world behaves in accordance with the rules of mereology. Immaterial table legs could still be part of immaterial tables, two immaterial roads could still overlap at the immaterial intersection, trigonometry would still be part of mathematics, and so on. We can still wonder whether parthood is transitive, reflexive, and asymmetric, even if the world is immaterial. Again: mereology is one thing, ontology is another.

1.2.4 Topic Neutrality and Univocality

A relation or property is *topic neutral* if it can be instantiated by an object of any ontological category. We tend to think that *similarity* is a topic-neutral relation: two chairs can be similar because they have the same shape and size, as can their shadows; two animals can be similar because they behave in the same kinds of ways; ideas can be similar because they express the same kind of thought; arguments can be similar because they share a particular formal structure; events can be similar because of the kinds of things that happen in each; historical enlightenment periods can be similar because they give rise to notable scientific and artistic advancements, and so on.[20] In contrast, properties such as *being a colleague* or relations such as *being taller than* cannot be instantiated by objects of any ontological category. Human beings who work together can be colleagues, but couches, cars, tennis shoes, and dinosaurs cannot. Objects that are spatially extended can be taller than other objects that are spatially extended, but abstract entities such as ideas, sets, numbers, or temporally extended events such as baseball games, ballets, and poetry slams cannot.

A predicate or term is *univocal* if it has the same meaning across contexts. Ordinary language terms such as 'ran' are notoriously equivocal, and can change meaning across uses. Compare "she ran a race" and "she ran a business." While the meanings of 'ran' are related, there is a clear difference in meaning – in the one

---

[20] For further discussion, see Uzquiano (2006) and McDaniel (2010a).

case, 'ran' picks out a physical exercise involving running shoes, whereas the latter involves organizing finances, directing employees, or having a limited liability company. Technical terms used in formal systems such as logic and set theory are given strict definitions in an effort to avoid ambiguity. The identity predicate and the existential quantifier are often supposed to be univocal.[21]

Topic neutrality and univocality are often seen as two sides of the same coin: there's the *metaphysical claim* about what the relevant relation or property is like or what kinds of things can instantiate it, and the *linguistic claim* about how the predicate behaves in statements or utterances. Generally, these track: predicates that are univocal pick out relations or properties that are topic neutral, and (we hope) the same for the other way around.

Yet even if a relation is topic neutral, it may apply to different things in different ways. McDaniel (2010a) explains that just because a relation is highly general or topic neutral, it doesn't follow from this that there aren't different modes or ways of being a part. One could think that there is only one *fundamental* parthood relation, which is consistent with thinking that there are a bunch of different kinds of nonfundamental parthood relations, each of which is definable in terms of the fundamental relation. *Compositional monism* is the view that there is one fundamental parthood relation.[22] *Compositional pluralism* is the view that there is more than one fundamental composition relation. Whether compositional monism or pluralism is true or whether there are nonfundamental parthood relations in addition to any fundamental one(s) will not be topics explored here. (I will be *assuming* compositional monism, for reasons I explain in a moment, but I won't argue for this claim.)

Wondering whether our ordinary parts–whole talk is univocal or topic neutral may initially strike us as a futile inquiry. Since mereology is a formal system, the relevant terminology can simply be *stipulated* to be unambiguous; we can define our parts–whole concepts as carefully and generally as we please. Yet classical extensional mereology takes at least one mereological concept as a theoretical primitive – in our case, 'part.' It is thus *undefined*. Related concepts – overlap, disjointedness, etc. – are defined in terms of it. This is why it is crucial that 'part' is univocal and intuitive. If it wasn't, it would be an inadequate primitive.

Sentences such as 1–16 are generally used to convince us that expressions such as 'part' in English can refer to a wide variety of portions of reality, and that such expressions are topic neutral and univocal. But not everyone holds this view. Mellor (2006) appeals to the following examples:

---

[21] Although see Hofweber (2009), McDaniel (2009, 2013), and Hirsch (2011).

[22] There may also be the assumption that the one fundamental composition relation is mereological. See Uzquiano (2006).

> The proposition that p is a part of the proposition that p&q.
> The property F is a part of the property F&G.
> The set of women is a part of the set of human beings.
> New South Wales is a part of Australia.
> The Terror was a part of the French Revolution.

He then observes:

> Notice . . . how heterogeneous this list is. The entities that it says are related as
> parts to wholes are pairs, respectively, of propositions, properties, sets,
> geographical regions, events and things. But equally striking, given this
> heterogeneity, is the homogeneity of each pair. In none of them is the
> whole different in kind from the part. Properties and propositions are not
> paired with each other, geographical regions are not paired with sets, things
> are not paired with events, and so on. (2006: 140)

Because of this (along with some other reasons), Mellor proposes that parts–
whole relations generally relate entities of the same kind, but that because there
are different kinds, our parts–whole concepts are *not* topic neutral. Similarly,
Simons (1987) maintains there are several different meanings of 'part,' each of
which depends on the metaphysical makeup of the alleged composers:

> There are different senses of 'part' according to whether we are talking of
> a relation between individuals, between classes, or between masses . . .
> [Extensional part–whole theories] have several different, but analogous,
> applications. The connections between the different analogous senses of
> 'part' . . . are sufficient to prevent there from being a single, overarching
> sense of 'part' which covers all of them, despite their appealing formal
> parallels. (128)

To put my cards on the table, I am sympathetic to the view that 'part' is either
equivocal or topic specific – in fact, it is a conclusion I support in Wallace
(2021). Nonetheless, I will assume in what follows that 'part' is topic neutral,
univocal, and that compositional monism is true. I do this for a few reasons.
First, since Lewis' *Parts of Classes*, this has been a standard assumption, so it is
worth taking it on to see what the consequences are.[23] It will also simplify our
discussion, allowing us to focus on other topics. Additionally, if we deny that
our parts–whole terminology is univocal, then we may need to deny that our
existential claims and quantifiers are univocal as well. Since mereology is in the
business of telling us how things compose, it is also in the business of telling us
how things exist *as composites*. If the way that a table leg is part of a table is

---

[23] Lewis (1991) remarks that his own view, whereby mereology is taken to be "perfectly understood, unproblematic, and certain" is a "minority opinion." It's not a minority opinion any longer,
in large part due to Lewis (1991).

different than the way in which the shadow of a table leg is part of the shadow of a table, then perhaps the way that a composite table exists is different than the way that the composite shadow of the table exists. If there are different ways of *being whole* or *being a part*, then perhaps there are different ways of *being*, full stop.[24]

Relatedly, if *similarity* and *identity* are assumed to be univocal and topic-neutral, it seems *parthood* should be, too. If we have a highly general, unified notion of identity, such that everything is identical with itself, and if, in accordance with the assumptions of mereology, identity is the limiting case of *parthood*, then it is plausible that we have a highly general and unified notion of *parthood* as well.

Most importantly, however, if one of the aims of mereology is to capture the basic rules and structure that govern our concepts of parts and wholes, then we should consider how we in fact think about things gathered into unities. We do, in fact, have the ability to think about any random things we please and consider them as one – as a collection, a group, a combined whole. We can name this collection, we can talk about it, we know which things are part of it and which are not, etc. The fact that we have a way of doing this – that we can generalize this process and come up with entirely new collections that we've never encountered before – is an argument in favor of our parts–whole concepts being highly general and unified.

1.3 Plurals

One of the assumptions made in Section 1.2.1 was the ability to refer to some things – in particular, the parts – plurally. But this is not allowed in standard classical first-order logic, which only contains singular constants, variables, quantifiers and predicates.[25] To illustrate, suppose the following claims are true:

17. There is a chair.
18. There are more particles than chairs.
19. Some particles are arranged chair-wise.
20. No particle is arranged chair-wise.
21. Some particles circle only one another.

---

[24] Cards on the table again: I am not entirely convinced that this consequence is so absurd. So I don't quite feel the force of this modus tollens as others might. Yet discussion of these issues would take us way too far afield. So I'll assume – what is currently a standard position in the literature – that there aren't different ways of *being*, or different ways of *being a part*. However, see McDaniel (2009, 2010a, 2013, 2017) for excellent discussions of these issues and an exploration of alternatives.

[25] Classical first-order logic is a predicate calculus involving quantifiers, truth functional connectives, and predicates. General familiarity with it is assumed here. For an accessible introduction and discussion, see another Element: Shapiro and Kissel (2022).

In classical first-order logic, we use singular quantifiers such as "∃x" and "∀x" to represent "there is an *x*" and "for all *x*," respectively. These quantifiers range over only singular objects in our domain. Sentence 17 above, for example, might be represented by (17*), where the predicate "is a chair" is represented by "C":

(17*) $\exists x(Cx)$

If we try to quantify over more than one object in classical predicate logic, like we might think is needed to adequately represent sentence 18, we may wind up saying something that isn't quite the expression we're looking for. We could quantify over the *number* of particles and the *number* of chairs, and then say something like, "The number of particles is greater than the number of chairs." Yet given our Quinean criterion of ontological commitment, this seems to commit us to *numbers*. For any of us with nominalistic leanings – i.e., anyone reluctant to admit abstract entities such as numbers into our ontology – this is quite an extraordinary consequence when all we wanted to do was talk about particles and chairs. Sentence 18 doesn't mention numbers at all.

Even leaving sentence 18 aside, sentence 19 will be even more difficult to capture, especially given the truth of 20. Sentences 19 and 20 are certainly compatible: some particles can be arranged chair-wise, even if no individual particle is arranged chair-wise itself. We understand that some things (plural) may have a property collectively (or taken together) that those same things don't have individually. You and I together can lift a couch even if you and I individually cannot lift a couch. Some may argue that this is an argument for appealing to collections, sets, classes, or mereological sums. Perhaps you and I cannot individually lift a couch, but the mereological sum of you and me can. If we have some particles that are collectively chair-shaped but individually not chair-shaped, then perhaps it is the mereological fusion of the particles that is chair-shaped. This is a way to interpret sentence 19 as 'there is a fusion of the particles that is chair-shaped' that is consistent with an interpretation of 20 as 'for any individual particle, it is not chair-shaped.' But intuitively, the subject of sentence 19 is not a mereological sum or fusion (or set or group) at all. The subject is just 'some particles,' and we need a way of expressing this, without bringing in sums, sets, or unities, which are not mentioned in the sentence.

Finally, sentence 21 is a version of a Geach-Kaplan sentence. It intuitively means something like: there is a collection of particles, each particle of which circles particles only in that collection and no particle that isn't in that collection, and no particle circles itself. Imagine that our domain (the things in our universe) contains only particles. And let's follow our strategy earlier (Section 1.2.2) by letting "X" refer to "the *xs*" *plurally* and "y ≼ X" to represent an inclusion predicate "*y* is one of the *X*" (both of which we'll discuss in a minute). Let "Cxy" stand for "*x* circles *y*." Then we can adequately express (21*) as:

(21*) $\exists X \forall y \forall z ((y \preccurlyeq X \ \& \ Cyz) \rightarrow (z \preccurlyeq X \ \& \ y \neq z))$

Yet (21*) is not equivalent to any sentence in classical first-order logic.[26] For these reasons (and others) we need a plural language and the ability to talk about some things plurally, without this talk or these expressions being grammatically reducible to our singular talk. We've already done this to some extent with our definition of 'fusion' and as a way to capture the Geach-Kaplan sentence (21). Our plural logic will contain plural variables ('*X*' for 'the *xs*,' '*Y*' for 'the *ys*,' etc.), plural constants, plural quantifiers, and two logical predicates: plural identity and an inclusion predicate.

A plural identity predicate allows plural terms in its argument places. In standard first-order logic, the identity predicate '=' takes only singular terms in its argument places: Superman = Clark Kent, Cassius Clay = Muhammad Ali, and so on. A plural identity predicate allows us to express plural identity claims such as: the Beatles = John, Paul, George, and Ringo; the bananas = the items in my cart; and so on. The plural terms in use in these examples are intended to be *irreducibly* plural. It is not that there are some things, the Beatles, that we individually quantify over and say something like, 'That one Beatle is identical to John, and this one identical to Paul, another George, and another Ringo.' Rather, the term 'the Beatles' is a plural term that refers plurally to some *things*, and these things are identical to John, Paul, George, and Ringo taken together. Our plural identity predicate allows us to express one–many and many–many identity claims, without reducing the many to singular things.

We also need an inclusion predicate, which we introduced above with our definition of 'fusion.' This predicate allows us to say that something is included among some other things; it helps us express a relation that something has to many. As before, we will let '*y* ≼ X' represent '*y* is one of X,' which expresses that there are some things, X, that *include* a singular thing, *y*.[27]

We have no need for a full semantics here.[28] It is enough for our purposes to recognize that a plural logic behaves just as classical singular logic, except that

---

[26] See Boolos (1984) for a discussion of the proof (credited to Kaplan). See also Linnebo (2022), endnote 2.

[27] In the literature, 'is one of' is most commonly used, but predicates such as 'among' or 'included in' are also used. Because 'is one of' is most common, and because many objections to composition as identity rely upon it, that's what we will use here.

[28] For that, see Boolos (1984, 1985), McKay (2006), Yi (2005, 2006), Oliver and Smiley (2016), and Linnebo (2022).

it allows us to quantify over objects plurally and say of these things that certain claims are true of them. It allows us to have a distinction between distributive predicates and collective predicates.

2 Composition and Decomposition

The chair you are sitting on is composed of a seat and some legs. At some point, the seat and legs were separated and the chair had yet to be assembled. So when, exactly, did it come into existence? Was it the moment the parts came together? The moment the screws were tightened? If I loosen a screw now, am I sitting on something that is flickering in and out of existence? If not, then when do the parts *compose* the chair? More generally, *When is there something composed of other things?* This is Peter van Inwagen's Special Composition Question (SCQ): "When is it true that: ∃y the xs compose y?" (van Inwagen 1990: 30).

To be clear, by "the xs compose y" van Inwagen specifically means "the xs are all parts of y and no two of the xs overlap and every part of y overlaps at least one of the xs." For comparison, our definition of fusion says that *w is a fusion of xs* if and only if *w overlaps all and only those things that overlap whatever is one of the xs*. So the crucial differences between 'the *x*s compose *y*' and 'the *x*s make a fusion, *y*' are whether we are including or excluding *x*s that overlap each other. In what follows, we will do likewise: when we talk about composite objects, we ignore overlapping parts.

We should also note that van Inwagen asks this question in the context of an inquiry about *material objects*, not objects *full stop.* By 'material object,' van Inwagen means something that "occupies space and endures through time and can move about in space (literally move about, unlike a shadow or wave or a reflection) and has surface and has mass and is made of a certain stuff or stuffs" (1990: 17). Our purpose will be to ask this question as wide open and generally as possible: when do *any* things compose something? We do not restrict our attention to material objects, or to things that are only spatio-temporally extended, causally efficacious, or things that can move about on their own. We want to leave all assumptions about kinds aside (for now). So we will understand the SCQ as follows: quantifiers completely unrestricted, when do any things *compose* something? There are three typical answers: *always, never,* and *sometimes.*[29]

---

[29] There are also a range of responses that might be best categorized as "it's complicated," such as compositional fictionalism or ontological deflationism, which we unfortunately do not have the time to explore here. See Dorr and Rosen (2002) for fictionalism, and Carnap (1950), Hirsch (2011), and Thomasson (2017) for various kinds of deflationism.

2.1 Always

Our *unrestricted fusion* axiom of mereology suggests a direct answer SCQ: *always*. This is also one of our explicit assumptions in the odd universe argument.[30]

UNRESTRICTED COMPOSITION: for any things whatsoever, there is an object composed of these things.

A *universalist* is someone who accepts *unrestricted composition*. One advantage of being a universalist is that we get to keep our commitment to the ordinary objects that ordinary intuition says that there are, which (as we will see) is a challenge for the 'never' views. Another is that we don't have to plunk down for an answer that is arbitrary, anthropocentric or ad hoc, which (as we will see) is a challenge for the 'sometimes' views. Accepting universalism also provides elegant solutions to a number of metaphysical puzzles – including worries about change over time, persistence, coincidence, and colocation.[31]

However, one of the primary complaints against universalism is that even though we get to keep our commitments to the ordinary objects that ordinary intuition says that there are, we have to accept too many extraordinary objects that ordinary intuition says that there *aren't*. For any things we have, the universalist claims we have a mereological sum of those things. In a world with just a coffee mug and a running shoe, we have the mereological sum of the mug and the shoe. In a world with just two souls, we have the mereological sum of these two souls. Universalists claim that any mereological sums are composite objects in the same sense. The mereological sum of a mug and a shoe and the mereological sum of two souls are both *things* composed of parts in the same sort of way. This is not only ontologically *quantitatively* explosive, some might argue, it is also *qualitatively* explosive. Reminiscent of our discussion just a moment ago (Section 1.2.3), we might wonder whether an 'always' answer not only entails that there are many more things than we thought there were, but also many more *kinds* of things.[32]

Pressing the point further, there are not just quantitative and qualitative explosions of material objects, there are quantitative and qualitative explosions of *everything* – all of the objects – that we think exist. If we have a mix of

---

[30] As mentioned earlier (n14), I am introducing 'unrestricted fusion' and 'unrestricted composition' separately. The former is an axiom of a formal system about parts and wholes, the latter concerns the relation that holds between some things (the parts) and another (the composite whole). It is an open question whether these notions are equivalent.

[31] We discuss issues of coincidence, persistence, and change only occasionally in what follows. For much more on these topics, see, e.g., Korman (2015, 2020b), Sattig (2021), and Wasserman (2021).

[32] Sattig (2021) calls the worry about qualitative explosiveness the 'strangeness objection,' and the worry about quantitative explosiveness the 'economy objection.'

abstract and concrete things in our ontology, then if universalism is true, we have all the sums that result from all of the combinations of these abstract and concrete things, as well as any sums that result from all combinations of any parts of these abstract and concrete things. Suppose that in addition to cats, mugs, and running shoes, we have the property of *being human*, the set of blue things, and the number two. According to universalism, we also have the mereological sum of the set of blue things and your cat's right paw, the sum of my coffee mug and the number two, and so on. If having to countenance mereological sums of trees and dogs is objectionable (Korman 2015: 27), then surely having to admit the sum of *being human* and half a cat is even more so!

To add to our worries is the recognition that mereology doesn't make any claim about which mereological sums (if any) are ordinary objects. If we already accept that there are some particles arranged chair-wise, then according to mereology, there is a mereological sum of the particles arranged chair-wise. Yet it is a further claim to say that this mereological sum *is* in fact the chair. *Colocated* or *coincident* objects are whenever more than one object is exactly occupying the exact same place at the exact same time. The mereological sum of the particles arranged chair-wise is exactly located where the chair is, at the exact same time. If the mereological sum is *not* identical to the chair, then there is both the mereological sum of particles, and the chair, exactly colocated. What goes for the chair goes for any other object. So, coincidence is everywhere.[33]

Moreover, it seems we have reasons to distinguish ordinary objects from mereological sums, if we think that mereological sums have their parts essentially. Perhaps we think that mereological sums cannot lose their parts or gain new ones and survive, yet ordinary objects can, which gives us a reason to think that no mereological sum is an ordinary object. Yet if we do not identify at least some mereological sums with ordinary objects, then on top of all of the ordinary tables and chairs, we *also* have all of the mereological sums. This is not only ontologically excessive but explanatorily impotent. If we've taken on all of these sums and *haven't* identified any of them with any ordinary objects, then our ontology is not only ontologically explosive, it is pointlessly so.

Taking this last worry first, the universalist could identify some of the mereological sums with ordinary objects, despite the initial implausibility in doing so. The mereological sum of all the particles arranged chair-wise, exactly located where my chair is, just *is* the chair. The mereological sum of the (hard copy) pages of this book, together with some glue and binding, just *is* a

---

[33] See van Inwagen (1981, 1990) and Merricks (1999) for arguments along these lines. See Wallace (2014a) for one kind of reply.

(hard copy) of this book. Then, as one option, the universalist could deny that mereological sums have their parts essentially. She could argue that mereological sums have their parts essentially only if we assume that a mereological sum is identical to its parts. If we deny that composition is identity, however, then it is not clear that a sum has its parts essentially. A sum could change its parts and survive, it could be identified with ordinary objects, and coincident worries would dissolve.

Alternatively, a universalist could embrace mereological essentialism, and assuage our worries by broadening the scope of what counts as 'parts' of an object. If ordinary objects are a combination of spatial, temporal, and modal parts, for example, then the way in which an object would have its parts essentially may align with our ordinary intuitions about change and persistence.[34] Admittedly, this move (along with the previous one) has been presented rather quickly and requires further metaphysical commitments on behalf of the universalist. But our purpose here is merely to show that the universalist has options.

As for concerns about universalism being wildly unparsimonious, we saw earlier (Section 1.2.3) that one way of ascertaining our ontological commitments is to look at the stuff before us and take an inventory, via *count*. We tally up all of the ontologically unsuspicious things, first, and then see if the suspicious entities are additional items in our domain. If they aren't, then parsimony is preserved. One straightforward way to do this is to claim that composition is identity. (This is my preferred option, but since it is not a view that is commonly endorsed, and there are many widespread objections to address, we'll save a longer discussion of this view for Section 3.) Other ways to do this are to assume that mereological sums are supervenient upon, or reducible to, or somehow or another already included in all of the stuff that we have prior to adoption of sums. One could lean heavily on some of the discussion we had earlier concerning the ontological innocence of mereological sums and insist that all of the extraordinary sums that a universalist is committed to are unproblematic. Sums are redundant given the existence of the parts; they come along for free, preserving parsimony.

Some may object that even if we have somehow addressed the worry about *quantitative* explosiveness, we still have not addressed the worry about *qualitative* explosiveness. Perhaps it is not the *number* of things that unrestricted composition commits us to, but the *kinds* of things that would result that are so egregious. Take a world with only a coffee mug and a running shoe.

---

[34] More on this kind of move in Section 3.3.2.

A universalist claims that in addition to the mug and shoe, there is also the mereological sum of the mug and shoe, *mugshoe*. Never mind that mugshoe might be an additional thing, distinct from the mug, distinct from the shoe. What kind of thing is it? It isn't a mug, for no mug has a part that's a shoe. Yet it isn't a shoe either, for no shoe has a part that's a mug. So what is it?

Again, a universalist might insist on the ontological innocence of mereological sums. By definition, a sum is just the thing (whole) that results when it has some things as parts. The only properties or features it has are inherited from the parts, which are features that we already had in our domain. Lewis (1991: 80) puts the point this way:

> It is no problem to describe an unheard-of fusion. It is nothing over and above its parts, so to describe it you need only describe the parts. Describe the character of the parts, describe their interrelation, and you have *ipso facto* described the fusion. The trout-turkey in no way defies description. It is neither fish nor foul, but it is nothing else: it is part fish and part foul. It is neither here nor there, so where is it – Partly here, partly there. That much we can say, and that's enough. Its character is exhausted by the character and relations of its parts.

Lewis himself embraces (a kind of) composition as identity; he claims that fusions just *are* their parts. However, one need not embrace composition as identity to endorse this particular response to the qualitative worry. Rather, all that's needed is an acceptance of the mereological definition of sum or fusion, and an understanding of wholes entirely in terms of their parts. In our world with only a mug and a shoe, the mereological sum mugshoe is neither a mug nor a shoe. Rather it is partly a mug and partly a shoe. We ordinarily understand what it is for some object to partly have a feature and to partly have another feature. A flag that is half white and half green is neither white nor green – it is partly white and partly green. So, there is no need to worry about the *kinds* of things that mereological sums deliver: they will inherit their features from their parts, which are objects we already accept.

I suggested earlier that mereology seems to capture how we in fact think about parts and wholes. We *do* have the ability to think of any random things we please as a group or whole or sum, and this is some reason to think that the axioms and definitions of mereology are getting something right. But if so, then not only does universalism seem to plausibly follow, none of the resulting sums seem all that extraordinary in either quantity or kind. Any worries about explosive ontologies seem to dissipate as soon as we take seriously what mereology says that sums *are* – namely, nothing more or less than the parts that compose them. Moreover, understanding sums in this way seems to render universalism fairly appealing and plausible.

Korman (2015: 16) addresses a similar line of reasoning for universalism, which he calls the *argument from assortments*.

(AS1) For any objects, there is an assortment or pair that has them as parts.
(AS2) If so, then for any objects, there is a single object composed of them.
(AS3) If so, then universalism is true.
(AS4) So, universalism is true.

If we think of sums as nothing more than assortments, then we have a straightforward argument from sums to universalism.

Korman responds to this argument by denying (AS2). He claims that 'assortment' does not pick out a single object, even though the term itself is grammatically singular. Rather, it refers to some things *collectively* and functions as a plural term. In addition, Korman claims that 'part' is not univocal. So the way in which a table leg is part of a table is different from the way in which a scraggly bird feather is part of the assortment of things collected by my toddler this morning. For Korman, the latter use of 'part' expresses the "amongness" relation, whereas (it is assumed) the former is not.

While I won't be arguing here about whether 'part' is univocal (I merely assume it, for reasons I gave earlier), I do think Korman's discussion about assortments is worth some attention. Perhaps our mereological terms 'sum' or 'fusion' behave similarly to Korman's understanding of 'assortment.' Do terms such as 'sum' and 'fusion' express the 'amongness' relation? Are they grammatically singular but referentially plural?[35]

In response to the first question, the answer is *yes*. The very definition of 'fusion' in mereology uses an inclusion predicate. Something w is a *fusion* of some things, X, when w overlaps exactly those things that overlap something that *is one of* the X. We introduced our definition using the predicate 'is one of,' but we could have also used 'among' or 'included in.' So, yes, the mereological notion of 'part' – or 'fusion' – explicitly includes appeal to an 'amongness' relation. This is what makes mereological sums so intuitive and appealing. Moreover, if a universalist is going to identify some of the available mereological sums with ordinary objects, then the way in which a table leg is part of a table will involve the inclusion predicate, too.

---

[35] See Simons (1987: 141–169) who distinguishes between *syntactic* and *semantic* plural terms. A term is semantically plural if it is referentially plural – i.e., it designates more than one object. Applying Korman's response to mereological sums, we could put the charge this way: 'sum' in mereology is syntactically singular but semantically plural, so mereology can not do the work it sets out to do. See also Cotnoir (2013) for discussion.

As for the second question, can we verify that 'sum' and 'fusion' are genuinely referentially singular, and not just grammatically singular but referentially plural, as Korman claims? I'm not entirely sure what evidence we can bring to bear when the worry is whether our language and metaphysics are coming apart. Usually, we use our linguistic evidence to guide our metaphysics; the challenge here is to consider the consequences of them being unaligned.

One option is to consider how the thing (or things) in question *behave*. Not how we talk about them and what we can say, but what they can *do*. We have something(s) in front of us, and we want to know whether it is a singular thing or many things. Is there something that many things can do that one thing cannot?[36] Perhaps. Recall our Geach-Kaplan sentence from Section 1.3:

21. Some particles circle only one another.

This sentence is usually used to make a grammatical point: the sentence cannot be translated using only singular quantifiers and expressions. But we could also consider the metaphysical implications, assuming the sentence is true. Some things (plural) can circle only one another, but a single thing cannot. So can a *sum* (or *fusion* or assortment) circle only one another? Ignore the ungrammaticality of it. Is it metaphysically possible? To my mind, it's not just that I have difficulty expressing this grammatically; I have difficulty imagining that this is something a sum can *do*. But this shouldn't be the case if 'sum' is genuinely referentially plural. If 'sum' is referentially plural, then the things that it picks out should be able to engage in plural activities.

I don't consider this point to be decisive, but I do think it pushes the debate a smidge further. What exactly is our test or evidence that a term is grammatically singular but referentially plural, aside from mere say-so? The suggestion on the table is: let's think about what plural things can *do*, not what we merely say about them, and see if the activities they can participate in differ from what a singular thing can do. Then if the thing(s) before us can participate in these plural activities, they are many; if not, then it is one.

One final consideration before we move on. The universalist fully admits that, according to her view, there may be very many mereological sums. Yet it is one thing to claim that there are lots and lots of sums, it is another to claim that there are lots and lots of sums that we notice, think about, and are the ordinary objects we know and love. Importantly, the universalist doesn't add to our ontology of *ordinary* things. There aren't more tables or chairs or cats or running shoes than we tend to think that there are. Rather, she thinks there are

---

[36] Assuming for the moment that composition is not identity and that something(s) cannot be both many and one.

more of the extraordinary things that we tend not to think about – until we do. She provides an ontology to account for our thoughts and talk about any random things we like as a group or whole, whenever we choose to do so.

Earlier, I compared mereology with language and logic (Section 1.2). I pointed out that while there are many (infinitely many) sentences in language and arguments in logic that are technically well formed, only a small subset of these are ones that we use or care about. This doesn't make the unused or uncared-for sentences any less well formed, or any less instructive for the purposes of learning language or logic. Likewise, a universalist may argue that mereology – including a commitment to unrestricted sums! – gives us the tools to think of a wide range of objects (wholes), even if only a small subset of these are ones we in fact use or care about. The universalist never said that the weird, unheard of objects were the ordinary ones. Rather, many of them are just that: weird and unheard of – until they are needed or noticed. Then they may still be weird, but at least they will be heard of. Most of us ignore them most of the time and no harm is done (see Lewis 1991: 80). Nevertheless, says the universalist, they exist.

2.2 Never

Compositional nihilism is the view that things never compose. There are *no* composite objects whatsoever; it's a 'never' answer to SCQ. The nihilist may admit that there are mereological simples – objects with no proper parts. And each of these simples may be an improper part of itself. But there is nothing that is a fusion of some other things. There is nothing that has proper parts, each of which are nonidentical to the whole.[37]

Why would anyone think that *nothing* composes or that there are *no* parts? Isn't it just *obvious* this is false? Look around: your table has parts (four legs, one top, two drawers); this Element has parts (Section 2.2, page 31, the references section); our thoughts, moods, rooms, roads, course contents, coffee mugs, and running shoes all seem to be things with parts. We can name them, think about them, count them. For most of the material things we own, if a small bit of it is broken or lost, we can buy a replacement part on Amazon. How could

---

[37] In the literature on composition, the term 'nihilist' is not always used consistently, or in the full-throttle unrestricted sense assumed here. Unger (1979a, 1979b) is often labeled a nihilist, yet he defends the view that there are no composite objects *that are subject to sorites of decomposition paradoxes*. Composites that are *not* subject to such paradoxes – such as certain subatomic particles, crystalline structures, water, gold, etc. – are acceptable. Peter van Inwagen (1990) and Merricks (2001) are also often considered nihilists (or eliminativists), yet they, too, have exceptions: in particular, when something is *living* or *a human being*. Sider (2013) comes close but softens his view at the end to not quite embrace it unrestrictedly.

this way of seeing the world – a way that doesn't seem to be all that complicated or confusing – be mistaken?

One of the main reasons to adopt such a seemingly counterintuitive view is because doing so solves so many philosophical problems. Go back to the odd universe argument for a minute. If we deny that anything ever composes, then any worry about how many objects there are dissolves into a worry about how many mereological simples there are – which, we might think, is not really a worry at all. How many objects are in the universe? "I don't know," says the nihilist, "but what I do know is that if we start with a finite number of simples, we can't then construct an a priori argument to the conclusion that there must be an odd number of things!" To the extent that we find the odd universe argument perplexing, this is certainly an argument in favor of nihilism: it (dis)solves the odd universe puzzle.

Other philosophical worries involve coincident objects and causal overdetermination. Let's assume for a moment that if there are any composite wholes, the parts are distinct from the whole. A nihilist will grant that there are lots and lots of simples (let's assume). The universalist does, too. But the universalist thinks there are wholes composed of simples, whereas the nihilist does not. In fact, *any* view where composite objects are admitted – any view that's not full-throttle nihilism – will be one where there are at least some wholes *in addition* to the simples. But then anywhere we have a composite object, the whole and the parts are exactly colocated, resulting in rampant coincidence. With rampant coincidence, comes rampant causal overdetermination. Suppose we have some simples arranged baseball-wise. The simples (collectively) cause the window to break; the (whole) baseball causes the window break. Yet if the simples are distinct from the whole, then whenever the parts cause something, the whole does, too. Overdetermination abounds (Merricks 2003: 56).

Nihilism resolves both of these puzzles in the same way: there are no objects composed of parts. If there are no composite objects, there is nothing for the simples to be coincident *with*, and nothing to *over*determine whatever the simples determine.

In addition to solving many philosophical puzzles, nihilism is also extremely ontologically and ideologically parsimonious. All of the worries about ontological explosion – both quantitative and qualitative – in response to universalism may lead us to looking for a theory that posits the *least* number of things, and the least number of *kinds* of things. If there are no composite objects, then there are just the fundamental bits: mereological simples. All that there is are the smallest things that cannot be broken down into further parts, because there are no such things as parts. It is also ideologically simple. We introduced mereology by taking 'part' as a theoretical primitive. It is undefined, and thus an ideological burden. According to nihilism, there are no parts, and thus no need for any such theoretical primitive (Sider 2007, 2013).

Despite all of these advantages, however, one of the primary objections to this view is a return to our initial reaction to it: it just *sounds* completely unintuitive. Philosophers can think about objects and the universe all they like, but if their resulting worldview from thinking about things from the armchair is that there are no armchairs, then the problem is likely with the thinking, not the world. While the universalist posits far too many objects, the nihilist posits far too few.

Nihilism also seems to entail rampant error theory about our everyday discourse of the world. If there are no cats or running shoes, then not only does this contradict our ordinary experiences, all of our utterances about our ordinary experiences are false. This is not only implausible (it certainly *seems* as if I am not saying false things all the time!), it leaves an explanatory gap as to how it is that we go around the world and get so much *done* – build bridges, drive cars, write papers – if bridges, cars, papers, and even we ourselves don't exist! And never mind the practical business of getting from one place to another, we can't even properly engage in science of any sort without molecules, atoms, chemicals, disease, medicine, defibrillators, clouds, mountains, atmospheres, planets, stars, galaxies, and so on.

It may be bad enough that nihilists deny that there are ordinary objects, or that all of our talk about ordinary objects is false, or that all of scientific inquiry is a sham. But there's more. Go back to our sentences 1–16. According to full-throttle nihilism, the first act of the play can't be the most boring part (there is no play that has parts), omniscience can't be part of god's nature (there is no godly nature that has certain properties as parts), trigonometry is not part of mathematics (there is no field of study that has subcategories as parts), moral codes don't have imperatives as parts, modal facts can't be part of our reasons for acting, and so on. So while the objection to nihilism is often made that, if nihilism is true, many of our ordinary claims about ordinary material objects are false, the problem is stronger than this. If compositional nihilism is true, there are no parts or composites *at all*, including parts of propositions, sentences, stories, plays, events, history, subjects, properties, ideas, assortments, moral codes, modality, and reasons.

Keep in mind our methodology. I had said at the outset that we would be employing a strategy of *cautious equilibrium* between common sense and philosophical theorizing. Yet notice that the considerations for nihilism (mentioned here) are all *theoretical* considerations. The odd universe, coincidence, overdetermination, parsimony – these are all *philosophical* worries. To get any of these puzzles or arguments off the ground, we have to take on highly (contentious) theoretical principles, first. We have to make an assumption about whether there are mereological simples, or what the composition relation is like, or whether coincidence is possible, or how one event causes another, or what prohibitions there must be for causes. In each case, it involves quite a bit of philosophical theorizing and a priori reasoning – any step of which could be questioned or contested. Against this, are our ordinary thoughts and talk about the world – thoughts and talk that not only seem mostly true most of the time, but also seems to account for how it is that we successfully get stuff done. Can we really be so sure that it is our abstract philosophical reasoning that is correct over our ordinary thoughts and talk? Can we really be more certain in a priori philosophical principles than we are certain that there's a table in front of us?

G. E. Moore (1959) is often attributed with endorsing the following principle: any premises used to argue for a counterintuitive view risks being undermined by our confidence in common sense. Lycan (2001: 39), in an effort to elaborate on this strategy, remarks that any "deductive 'proof' can be no more than an invitation to *compare plausibility.*" Any valid argument with premises $P_1, \ldots, P_n$ to some conclusion, C, can be reinterpreted as a claim that the set $\{P_1, \ldots, P_n, {\sim}C\}$ is inconsistent. This allows for two moves in response: we can either accept all of the premises and the anticommonsensical conclusion (as the nihilist wants us to do), or we can reject one of the premises and stand firm with common sense. In short, plunking down for common sense, and rejecting certain philosophical premises that conflict with common sense, is always a legitimate, available move. So, in response to the nihilist, we might insist that we are more certain that there are coffee mugs and running shoes than we are of any philosophical principles that might be used to argue to the contrary.

One way nihilists have responded to this Moorean move – and tried to assuage the seeming unintuitiveness of their view – is by offering a story about how our ordinary thoughts and talk about the world aren't as wildly false as they may appear. The nihilist may offer a *paraphrase* of ordinary object discourse to ensure that there isn't rampant error theory (van Inwagen 1990: 108–114). She may insist that many of the statements we in fact make are shorthand for the nihilist facts. Nihilists don't think that there are coffee mugs, cats, and running shoes, but they do think there are a bunch of simples arranged mug-wise, cat-wise, and shoe-wise. These simples arranged in various ways may look very similar to ordinary composite objects; they may have the same shape, the same weight, the same size, and so on. In fact, according to the nihilist, there is very little (if any) detectable, empirical difference between a nihilist world filled with simples arranged in various ways and the compositional realist world filled with composite objects. So, when we say things like "here is a coffee mug," the nihilist may insist that it is quite plausible that what we are *really* saying is "here are some simples arranged mug-wise." Since the empirical difference between these two options doesn't register visually, there is likely little detectable difference in terms of the content of what we say. In this way, our ordinary thoughts and talk aren't as wildly false as they may appear – rather, the *content* of our ordinary thought and talk is different than it may appear.

This will no doubt strike some of us as implausible. Shouldn't it be transparent to us (more or less) what we are saying and not saying? Don't we know whether we are talking about macrolevel composite objects or just a bunch of individually imperceptible simples arranged macro-object-wise?

In response, the nihilist may point out that we very often speak imprecisely, uncarefully, or loosely, and we don't always mean exactly what we say. "Look at that sunset!" we exclaim, knowing full well that the earth is round and not at the center of the solar system, and that the sun does not literally set. "It's raining and not raining," we say during a sunshower, both of us firm believers in the law of noncontradiction (cf. van Inwagen (1990: 101). Nonetheless, we somehow keep saying things and getting things done, even if the literal content of our utterances is not quite right. Likewise, the nihilist claims, we may be making utterances about composite objects, even if the literal facts of the world are nihilistic. This may be surprising, but – importantly! – it doesn't lead to rampant error theory.

Although just how a nihilist makes sense of *anyone speaking* – whether loosely or strictly or any which way – when, according to her own view, there are no people or speakers or utterances (for all of these things have parts!) is certainly puzzling. Some may even say: self-defeating. If one is a full-throttle compositional nihilist, then how can there even be people, utterances, thoughts, sentences, language, and perhaps even intensional content, since all of these are compositional in nature? How can a nihilist even launch her defense when a defense itself is composed of parts (premises, propositions, lemmas, conclusions, etc.)?[38] In light of these challenges, nihilism might strike some of us as a last resort.

2.3 Sometimes

A 'sometimes' answer to SCQ is often championed as the one that most aligns with common sense. For many, given the radical alternatives of universalism and nihilism, this is one of the primary considerations for thinking the 'sometimes' answer is the correct one. Call such a person a *compositional moderate*.[39]

---

[38] See, e.g., Sider (2013), although the position he endorses is not the extreme nihilism imagined here.

[39] Terminology from van Inwagen (1990: 61).

Unlike the universalist, the moderate doesn't posit too many objects; yet unlike the nihilist, she doesn't posit too few.

Of course, the devil is in the details. When, exactly, do some things compose and when, exactly, do they not? Perhaps some things compose whenever they are glued or fastened together, or are in an appropriate arrangement, or when the parts are close enough to each other or are in contact. These are all reasonable proposals for a 'sometimes' answer, each of which seemingly aligns with ordinary intuition about ordinary composite objects.[40] Yet finding the necessary and sufficient conditions for restrictions on composition is notoriously difficult – so difficult, we may conclude that it just can't be done.

Moreover, there are a whole battery of bizarre candidate conditions for composition, still within the bounds of qualifying as a 'sometimes' answer to SCQ, yet none of which align with common sense. Things could compose when they are dancing, or moving at a certain speed, or located in my office on a Tuesday, or just whenever god gives the official "ok." Surely, none of these proposals about when composition occurs would align with common sense. Just because a proposal may be a 'sometimes' answer, this doesn't automatically reap commonsense approval. Thus, while the three traditional answers to SCQ are certainly convenient and pithy – always! never! sometimes! – carving up the response space in this way leaves the middle ground of 'sometimes' too vast to be helpful and too varied to serve as a commensurate alternative to the extreme ends of 'always' and 'never' (cf. Fairchild 2021: 621).

A less elegant but more serviceable division of answers would be: *more often than we think, less often than we think, just about as often as we think.* This allows some of the more bizarre 'sometimes' views to be clumped with radical ends of universalism and nihilism, while allowing more moderate views that cohere with common sense to be more unified *because* they cohere with common sense. In what follows, I use 'compositional moderate' to indicate those who think that some objects compose *just about as often as we think.*

The primary objections to the moderate view are intertwined with and related to its advantages: ok sure, *because* the moderate view aligns with common sense, it passes the human standard. But why should we think that the human standard is so great? What is so special about us and how we see the world? We are contingent beings who make mistakes and have opinions that change on a whim. If we had been made just a little bit different – if we had been born being able to see the microscopic facts, or had X-ray vision, or saw things perpetually in pairs or triples – then different things would have mattered to us and *those*

---

[40] Of course, not always. See van Inwagen (1987, 1990).

things would have been the human standard. It doesn't seem that the metaphysical facts about which objects are in the world should be subject to mere contingent facts about how we are built or the outcome of our unprincipled opinions. In this way, using the human standard for composite objecthood seems arbitrary, anthropocentric, and ad hoc.[41] In short, it is the recognition of the fragility and inconsistency of our own opinions about what counts as an object and what does not that seemingly undermines using this as a metaphysical marker for when composition occurs (and when it does not).

Moreover, we often have a tolerance for small changes and an intolerance for big changes, yet the small changes often add up to the big changes, landing us in paradox.[42] As so many philosophical puzzles about ordinary objects seem to demonstrate, we just aren't very good at keeping our beliefs about ordinary objects free from contradiction. So, on the one hand, our own common opinion seems important enough that if a philosophical view is going to run wildly against it, we have reasons to object to the philosophical view under scrutiny. Yet, on the other hand, a view that kowtows to common sense must contend with the fact that human opinion about the world is contingent, fallible, and fluid.

But let's move on to a different point. This Element is particularly concerned with the odd universe argument, so let's articulate a worry for the moderate in terms of counting. First, let's recognize that compositional moderates reject unrestricted composition, and this is enough to get them out of the odd universe puzzle. Since unrestricted composition is one of our explicit assumptions, if it is false, the argument is unsound. So, the moderate won't conclude that there are an odd number of things in the universe. Done. (And some think: one more argument in favor of the moderate – hooray!)

Yet there is another counting argument waiting in the wings, similar in kind to the odd universe. According to the moderate, sometimes composition occurs and sometimes it doesn't – and we may not know or be able to articulate the conditions under which composition occurs or doesn't. Fine. But let's assume that, at some point, there are such conditions. Maybe it's not the exact number of small particles, but that they have to be arranged in the right way, or moving together with the right speed, or recognized by human beings or god to be worthy of objecthood. Whatever the conditions, call them C. And for

---

[41] I am admittedly blending together a whole family of arguments that are typically launched against the compositional moderate (and sometimes used as an argument *for* nihilism or universalism). It is worth parsing out the distinctions between these arguments; unfortunately, I do not have the space to do so here. See, e.g., Yablo (1987), Barnes (2007), Korman (2015, 2020a, 2020b), Fairchild and Hawthorne (2018), and Fairchild (2021), for more in-depth discussion.

[42] This is getting at vagueness and sorites puzzles, which I do not address here. See Hyde and Raffman (2018) for a nice overview and further references.

comparison, let's go through the odd universe argument again, slightly modified, with each of our positions in mind and how they will respond: the universalist, the nihilist, and the moderate.

We start with a world with one mereological simple in it, a. How many things are in this world? Intuitively one: a. The universalist says so, the nihilist says so, and the moderate says so. This is the one case on which they all agree. Now add a mereological simple to the world, b. How many objects are in this world? The universalist who rejects composition as identity says three, the nihilist says two, and the moderate (likely) says two. At this point, the universalist who thinks that composition is not identity is the only one who is committed to there being an odd number of things in the world, no matter how many mereological simples we add. The nihilist will say that there are an odd number of things whenever there are an odd number of simples; since there is no composition, we never get more objects than the number of simples.

The moderate is different. At some point, there are enough simples, arranged in the right way, moving at the right speed, or whatever conditions are specified in C. But there also has to be a certain number of simples. Call this N. When there are $N-1$ simples, according to the moderate, there are $N-1$ things in the universe. Yet as soon as we add one more simple (assuming conditions C hold), we do *not* get N number of objects in the universe. We *jump* from $N-1$ things to N *plus* however many objects the compositional moderate allows (given that there are the appropriate number of simples, and conditions C hold).

Suppose that conditions are right for there to be a cube, according to the moderate's own standards. A cube is made of parts – the left half of the cube, the right half of the cube, the top third, the bottom two thirds, lots of small particles, and so on. To simplify matters, let's assume there is only the cube, composed of the left half and right half of the cube, all of which are composed of N mereological simples. Let us also assume that composition is not identity. According to the moderate, at some point there are $N-1$ simples and no cube, and no left half or right half of the cube. Then at another point, there are N simples *and* a cube *and* a left half *and* a right half of the cube. When there are $N-1$ simples and no cube, there are $N-1$ things in the universe. When there are N simples, there is also a cube, and a left half and right half of the cube. So, when there are N simples, there are suddenly $N+3$ things!

To be clear, the incredulity is not just that we've gone from a world without a cube to a world with a cube by the addition of just one mereological simple. That's bizarre, I admit, but perhaps the moderate has made her peace with this. It's that we've gone from a world with $N-1$ many things to a world with $N+3$

things, when all we've added was one mereological simple! As soon as there are *N* simples, the cube – along with its right and left halves – pops into being. The moderate could reply that the right and left halves exist before the cube does. Yet if the halves of the cube exist before the cube does, how does one extra mereological simple make a difference to there being a cube? If the halves already exist, shouldn't the cube exist as well? Whatever the details the moderate gives to answer this question, it still seems that there needs to be an unjustified jump in the number of things.

To be clear, this isn't a worry about the conditions under which a particular ordinary object exists (or doesn't). This is a worry about how many things there are all across the board. Never mind whether there's a cube or not. How many things do we have, *full stop*? The moderate has to admit that at some point – whenever that is and whatever conditions she accepts – the addition of one mereological simple will force a jump from (i) the number of things in the universe being identical to the number of simples to (ii) the number of things in the universe being identical to the number of simples *plus* all of the composite objects. Because at some point, whenever that is, we cross the threshold from there not being composite objects to there being composite objects. In terms of how many objects there are, this just seems *weird*. Who knew that one lone simple can be so powerful? It dramatically amplifies the number of things in the universe (by more than just one)!

This worry is a version of an argument from vagueness against the moderate. But putting it in terms of the number of things that there are in the universe (to my mind) makes the point more palpable. It is incredibly hard for me to get into the mood that we go from there being, say, forty-nine things in the universe because we have forty-nine simples, to there being fifty-three things, because we added one mereological simple.

A moderate might reply that she doesn't commit to there being clear ontological cutoffs between there being a composite object and there not being a composite object. Perhaps she accepts ontic vagueness – that it is sometimes vague whether there is a composite table before us or not, and that this vagueness is in the *world*, instead of in our language or beliefs (Korman 2015). But the above example emphasizes the oddness of this position: by stipulation, it is not vague whether conditions C hold, or whether a single mereological simple is added, yet somehow it is a vague matter about how many things are in the world, because it is a vague matter as to whether something composes. But where is the vagueness? Is it in the composition relation? What exactly is the composition relation if it is subject to vagueness? It can't be a variation of identity or similarity or any logical relation or existence, unless we want to accept ontic vagueness about those, too. And whatever the answers are here, it seems that the moderate will be committed to saying that there will always (or: very often) be an indeterminate number of things.

The moderate has some options here, but unfortunately it would take us too far afield to explore them. It is perhaps enough for our purposes to leave the point as follows. It is not obvious that any option for the moderate will be more intuitive or less problematic than the worries for universalism and nihilism. According to universalism, the world has more things in it than we think there are – but that's ok, she says, because there are just lots of things that we don't notice or care about, and we can keep on not noticing or caring about them without disrupting normal life. According to nihilism, the world has far fewer things than we think there are – but that's ok, they say, because what's really there is close enough to what we thought was there so it doesn't make too much difference to what we ordinarily say and do. According to the moderate, in some ways, the world is just about the way that we think it is – there are just the sorts of things we think there are and not very many things we think that there aren't. Nonetheless, while the moderate may align with common sense about *which* objects exist, she doesn't seem to align with common sense about how many. That's certainly peculiar. Our world is either a lot *jumpier* or *fuzzier* than we thought, even in places where we expect precision.

When we introduced the odd universe argument, it was important to see that it wasn't the implausibility of the conclusion that was the source of the trouble, it was the *generalizability* of the argument that is so problematic. It can apply to any domain. It's an a priori argument that there are an odd number of things everywhere we look, whether that be in Kentucky or the sock drawer. Similarly, with the compositional moderate, either the world wildly jumps from there being some number of simples to a world with those simples plus all of the composites, or else indeterminism abounds. This isn't just a special case when we consider how many things are in the entire universe. Rather, the worry is that if the compositional moderate is right, there's jumpiness or fuzziness *everywhere we look*. It's not clear that this is much better than what the universalist and nihilist have to offer.

There is much more to say here. Yet I hope the above discussion gives a decent sketch of some of the basic issues, positions, and available moves with respect to composition and the three main answers to SCQ.

2.4 All the Way Down

We turn now to *decomposition*. As we have seen, *composition* is a bottom-up consideration: what happens when we start with some stuff, and build up from there, via composition? Decomposition is the reverse. It's a top-down consideration: what happens if we start with one big thing, and break it down, via decomposition?

Take the universe. The whole thing. Once we've got it, does it *decompose* into its smaller bits? How? If we have a table, can we cut it in half? Can we cut those halves in half? What if we keep going, ad infinitum? If our knives are too big and the pieces too small, can someone more powerful or with better tools do it? Is reality just parts all the way down? Or is there a point at which even an all-powerful being couldn't slice things up any further?

These questions lead us to one of our explicit assumptions in the odd universe argument:

SIMPLES: the universe is, at rock bottom, made up of finitely many mereo-logical simples.

If we deny that the universe is made up of finitely many mereological simples, what are the alternatives? One option is to claim that the universe is made up of *infinitely* many simples. Another option is to claim that there are no simples – that every part has parts, all the way down. A thing with parts all the way down is called *gunk*. Or we might think that the world is a mixture of simples and gunk. Let's look at some of these options below.

2.4.1 Infinite Simples

Suppose that we reject *simples* because we think that the universe is made up of *infinitely* many simples. That is, we don't deny that there are mereological atoms – things with no proper parts. Rather, what we deny is that there are only finitely many of them.

If we assume that the universe has infinitely many simples, then there are either *countably* or *uncountably* many simples. Some things are *countable* if they can be put in a one–one correspondence with the natural numbers $(1, 2, 3, 4 \ldots)$. Some things are *uncountable* if they can be put in a one–one correspondence with the real numbers $(1, \frac{1}{2}, \sqrt{3}, \pi/5 \ldots)$. Since the real numbers are a continuum, they cannot be put in a one–one correspondence with the natural numbers; there are more reals than natural numbers, even though both sets are infinite.[43]

If we reject *simples* because we think that the universe is made up of infinitely many simples, then in principle it seems we should have at least two genuine options: either there are countably or uncountably many things in the universe. However, if we assume that there are *countably* many simples, then classical extensional mereology - together with a full semantics and a comprehension principle - entails that the domain is the size of the power set of the natural numbers, which is uncountable. (see Cotnoir and Varzi 2021: 237 and 240–244) In other words, if we assume that there are countably many simples, there *cannot* be countably many objects. This is

---

[43] See Bagaria (2021) and Burgess (2022).

certainly surprising. (Some may say: unacceptable.) Whatever our reasons for thinking that the world is made up of infinitely many simples, it seems implausible that we *must* conclude – via an a priori argument – that there are uncountably many things. At least, it is not clear how this is any better than having to conclude a priori that there is an odd number of things. Let's see if there's another option.

2.4.2 Gunk

Another way to deny our assumption, *simples*, is to deny that there are any simples at all. Perhaps there are no smallest bits – things that, at rock bottom, cannot be divided any further. Perhaps it is just parts all the way down. A world of *atomless gunk*, where every part has proper parts (Lewis 1991: 20).

Imagine the table in front of you is sliced in half. Take one of those halves and slice it in half. Keep going. For every bit, imagine that it is sliced in half over and over, so that each half is halved. Eventually, we may need to cut with a smaller and smaller knife (no problem: just grab one that is half the size of the one previously used). And we may need to make our cuts half as quick if we want to avoid slicing forever (no problem: just make each cut half as quick as the cut before it). If you think that cutting like this is impractical, that's fine. The point is to imagine that the halving keeps going. If the world would in fact behave this way, it's gunk.

One might think that if the world is gunky, it rules out certain views on composition – namely, nihilism.[44] In a gunky world, everything has parts all the way down; there is no 'base level' of noncomposite things. Yet if, in a gunky world, there are no noncomposite things, yet the nihilist doesn't permit composite things, and things have to be either composite or noncomposite, then nihilism seems incompatible with gunk.

Perhaps this doesn't seem like much of a cost. After all, gunk is pretty weird. Isn't it a benefit of a view if it can definitely rule out weird things like gunk? Perhaps. Yet in this case – similar to our worries with the odd universe argument, and our concerns with countable or uncountable simples above – it seems implausible that an a priori argument could deliver a verdict one way or the other. Whether the universe is gunky doesn't seem to be the kind of thing that we can prove simply by thinking about things from the armchair. So, if nihilism rules out gunk a priori, so much the worse for nihilism.

A nihilist has some ways to respond, which we won't pursue here.[45] For our purposes, what matters is that we could deny *simples* in the odd universe

---

[44] See Sider (1993); for a reply, see Sider (2013).

[45] For further discussion, see, e.g., Sider (1993, 2011, 2013), Hudson (2007), van Cleve (2008), Effingham (2011), Markosian (2015), and Brzozowski (2016).

argument because we think that the world is gunky - either entirely or just in certain places. But then we would need not just an argument to show that gunk isn't ruled *out*, we would need an argument to show that at least some gunk is ruled *in*. That is, there's a difference between being open to gunk as a logical possibility and plunking down for gunk as the way that some (or perhaps all) of the world *is*. While I can see some motivation for allowing the possibility of gunk, I don't see what evidence one could bring for thinking gunk is actual.

2.4.3 Zeno

Zeno is attributed with giving at least two arguments against motion, on the assumption that the world has parts. If the world has parts, then it is either infinitely or finitely divisible. If it is *infinitely* divisible, no one can get or move anywhere.[46] Yet if it is *finitely* divisible, then (again) no one can get or move anywhere. Together, these are *a reductio ad absurdum* against the original assumption that the world has parts. If so, nihilism follows. Let's look at this argument in more detail.

The Racetrack. First assume that space and time are infinitely divisible. Imagine that Achilles is trying to get from his starting point, START, to some arbitrary end point, END. We begin with the assumption that Achilles can get *halfway* to END; call this halfway point H_1. Then we worry about how Achilles can get from H_1 to END. In order to get from H_1 to END, Achilles has to go halfway again, H_2. To get from H_2 to END, Achilles must go halfway yet again, H_3. And so on. Before Achilles can go from any halfway point to END, he must traverse half of that distance first. Since Achilles cannot make infinitely many journeys, he can never reach END. Since END is any arbitrary point whatsoever, the point generalizes: he never gets anywhere – i.e., Achilles can't move.

The Arrow. Next assume that space and time are *not* infinitely divisible. There are both *spatial* and *temporal minima* (or: simples). An arrow travels from point A to B. At any instant (*temporal minima*) the arrow is taking up only one region of space, an arrow-shaped region. During any instant, the arrow is at rest, for if it were moving, the instant would have parts. But if at every instant during the arrow's flight it is *not* moving, the arrow never moves. Suppose we've accounted for every instant. How does it change position and get from A to B? It doesn't. So, the arrow never moves.

The Racetrack entails that the world cannot have infinitely many parts, while the Arrow entails that the world cannot have finitely many parts. Since these are logically exhaustive options, it must be that the world has no parts.

---

[46] For discussion, see Salmon (2001) and Sainsbury (2009: Ch. 1).

1z.　Assume that the world has parts.

2z.　The world either has infinitely or finitely many parts.

3z.　Suppose it has infinitely many parts.

4z.　Then absurdities follow ("the Racetrack").

5z.　So suppose that it has finitely many parts.

6z.　Then absurdities follow ("the Arrow").

7z.　Either way, absurdities follow.

8z.　So, our assumption must be false; the world does not have parts.

Above I had asked how the universe *decomposes*. What happens when we break it down into ever smaller bits? Do we ever get to the smallest bits that have no parts? Or is it parts all the way down? The combined Zeno arguments are one answer: no matter how we slice it, absurdity awaits. So, there are no parts.

Interestingly, we can think of the odd universe argument as one horn of a similar dilemma, based on the same assumption that the world has parts. However, this time, we consider the consequence for *composition* not decomposition.

Assume that at rock bottom, the world is either simple or gunky. It either bottoms out in partless bits or it is parts all the way down. In a world of simples, there are either finitely or infinitely many simples. Assume that the universe has finitely many simples. Then if we count up all of the composite objects (and the odd universe argument is sound), we get the conclusion that there are an odd number of things in the universe. Alternatively, assume that the universe has infinitely many simples. Then there are either countably or uncountably many simples. Yet by reasoning similar to the odd universe argument, either way, there are uncountably many things in the universe. Putting the arguments together, if we assume that the world is a world of simples, then there are either an odd number of things in the universe or uncountably many. Either way seems absurd.

The alternative is gunk. Wherever the universe is gunky, then Zeno's Racetrack argument applies. But we may also worry about what this means for *composition*. Wherever the universe is gunky, is there ever an end to the objects that compose? If there are *parts all the way down*, are there *composite wholes all the way up*? A world is *gunky* if every object *has* a proper part. A world is *junky* if every object *is* a proper part.[47] Does having a gunky world lead one to a junky one? Wherever the world is gunky, how many composite objects should we expect? At least as many

---

[47] For more on gunk and junk, see, e.g., Markosian (2005), Bohn (2009a), (2009b), Dasgupta (2009), Schaffer (2010), Sider (2013), Cameron (2014), Cowling (2014), and Brzozowski (2016).

objects as there are parts: uncountably many! A gunky world is strange indeed, but certainly when we think about how many composite things it yields.

Like Zeno, we may take the above reasoning as a *reductio* on our original assumption that the universe has parts. So, there are no parts.

Does this mean we should resign ourselves to nihilism? Fortunately, no. Keep in mind that the problem with arguments such as the odd universe is not *just* the implausibility of the conclusion. Rather, it's that the reasoning is generalizable. The odd universe argument applies to any domain of any size, as do the assumptions used to generate it. The entire universe is a pretty big place to think about, so think smaller. Do we think that, at rock bottom, there are finitely many simples in Kentucky? In the sock drawer? On your desk? Or do we think that there are infinitely many things – either infinitely many simples or atomless gunk – *everywhere* we look? Putting things this way may help hone our intuitions. To my mind, it hones them in favor of *simples*.

But there's no need to overly commit ourselves. The odd universe argument only works if it's sound. So far, we've only looked at two of the required assumptions: *unrestricted composition* and *simples*. I think that we should grant both of these, as should be evident from our discussion up until this point. But I'm also willing to settle for a weaker conditional: *if* unrestricted composition and simples are true, the odd universe is (still) unsound. This is because one of the other assumptions – *composition is not identity* or *count* – is false. Let's take a look.

3 Identity and Counting

There are not very many who defend the claim that composition is identity – although the view is steadily gaining adherents.[48] For many, the differences between parts and wholes are simply too obvious and numerous for the view to be plausible. The parts are many, the whole is one. The parts are small, the whole is big. The parts are light, the whole is heavy. The parts can be scattered and survive, the whole cannot. The parts existed before the whole, the whole

---

[48] Cotnoir and Baxter (2014) provide an excellent overview and comprehensive collection of discussions on this topic. They, like many in the literature, discuss *composition as identity*, often abbreviated "CAI." This way of categorizing a range of views about composition is useful because it includes weaker versions where composition is not quite – but almost! – identity. Since I endorse a stronger version where composition *is* identity, I will stick with the abbreviation "CI" when discussing this variation. Finally, Payton (2022a) distinguishes between composition as identity (CAI) and composition entails identity (CEI). Composition entails identity is committed to the claim that $X = y$ if FyX. Composition as identity is often characterized as being committed to the stronger thesis that $X = y$ iff FyX. These distinctions, while important, do not matter for our purposes here. See also Payton (2021a and 2021b).

exists after the parts disappear. The whole can survive a replacement of its parts, the parts cannot survive a replacement of themselves. And so on.

Nonetheless, to see why some might initially be tempted by the claim that composition is identity, let's begin with one of Donald Baxter's examples (1988a: 579):

> Suppose a man owned some land which he divides into six parcels ... He sells off the six parcels while retaining ownership of the whole. That way he gets some cash while hanging on to his land. Suppose the six buyers of the parcels argue that they jointly own the whole and the original owner now owns nothing. Their argument seems right. But it suggests that the whole was not a seventh thing.

The idea is fairly straightforward. For any normal composite thing – some land and the parcels that compose it, a six-pack and its six individual beers, an Ikea cabinet and all of its packageable parts – we tend to think that if someone has all of the parts, they thereby have the whole. If Ikea ships all of the parts of a cabinet to me, it would be unreasonable for me to call customer service and complain that, while they certainly sent all of the parts and none of them are missing, they failed to send me the cabinet (cf. Casati and Varzi 2008: 68). The whole cabinet just *is* the parts; if I have the parts, I have the cabinet. There is certainly some intuitive pull for the view that composition is identity.

Of course, the details of how a rigorous philosophical view of composition could adequately capture this intuitive pull is up for some debate. There are at least three varieties of composition is identity that are endorsed or discussed in the literature:[49]

Weak CAI: the composition relation is *analogous* to identity.
Moderate CAI: the composition relation is *nonnumerical identity*.
Strong CAI: the composition relation is *numerical identity*.

In what follows, I aim to provide some considerations in favor of Strong CAI, which I'll simply call "CI." Not only is this a view that I personally prefer, and

---

[49] These categories are given in Cotnoir (2014b). Lewis (1991) is often attributed with endorsing *Weak CI*. He claims that while the parts are the whole, and the whole is the parts, composition is only "strikingly analogous to ordinary identity" (1991: 84). Armstrong (1978, 1997) might also be considered in this camp. Meanwhile, Cotnoir (2013) and Bricker (2016) endorse different kinds of *Moderate CI*, although for further debate see Bricker (2019). Bohn (2011), (2014), (2021), Wallace (2011a), (2011b), Payton (2021a, 2021b), and Payton (2022b) endorse various kinds of *Strong CI*. Baxter (1988a, 1988b, and 2014) endorses a kind of *Moderate CAI* but rejects the indiscernibility of identicals, leading to what Lewis has called a "stronger, and stranger" view (Lewis 1991: 84n12). Baxter (2014) himself embraces this characterization and calls it "Stranger Composition." See also Turner (2014), McDaniel (2014), and Calosi (2021).

defend elsewhere, it is the version of CAI that seems to glean the most advantages (Wallace 2011a, 2011b). Moreover, if CI can resist some of the arguments directed against it, then there will be fewer reasons to move to more moderate or weaker versions. That said, I do not have the space here to offer a full-blown defense of the view. The content below aims to show how, despite many objections, CI is a coherent philosophical position that deserves more serious attention than it typically receives. Our goal is to undermine *composition is not identity*, which might be accomplished by merely deflating the usual confidence that CI is obviously false.

3.1 Advantages of CI

One of the biggest advantages for CI is that it readily explains the intimate relationship between parts and wholes. Parts and wholes are often in the exact same location, doing the exact same sorts of things, behaving in the exact same sorts of ways. Parts and wholes completely and totally overlap. CI explains *why* this is so. It has a ready explanation as to why parts and wholes are metaphysically interdependent – they are identical (Cotnoir and Baxter 2014).

Additionally, embracing CI is one way to make universalism ontologically innocent. If the parts are identical to the whole, then whenever we have some parts, the whole literally comes along for free. As Lewis claims: they are it, it is them (1991: 83). All of our earlier worries about whether universalism is ontologically explosive dissipate if composition is identity.[50] Relatedly, CI nicely accounts for our intuitions about double counting of parts and wholes. When we order a cabinet from Ikea, we don't have to make a separate, additional purchase for the parts; if we did, that would be double counting (and double purchasing)! Embracing CI would give us a very straightforward explanation for *why* this is double counting: we are literally counting identical things twice.

Because CI is a rejection of one of the explicit assumptions in the odd universe argument, accepting CI also allows us to resist the unwanted conclusion. Even if universalism is true, if the mereological sum of *a* and *b*, *ab*, is identical to *a* and *b*, then we won't have three things in a world with just *a* and *b*. (Of course, just *how* exactly this will work will be spelled out more fully in Section 3.4.)

Accepting that composition is identity provides solutions to many metaphysical puzzles, especially ones involving coincidence and overdetermination. Earlier I had mentioned that if the universalist countenances composite sums

---

[50] See Cotnoir (2014b), Hawley (2014), Varzi (2014), and Bennett (2015) for different articulations of this claim. See Loss (2022) for some pushback.

in addition to the parts, then we may encounter rampant coincidence. Yet if the parts just *are* the whole, coincidence worries dissolve. Similarly, we won't have any overdetermination problems. If the parts just are the wholes, there's nothing distinct from the simples to overdetermine any effects.[51]

3.2 Leibniz's Law and Hybrid Identity

As we will see in a minute, many of the challenges for CI involve Leibniz's Law – a principle that we will assume a CI theorist aims to preserve:

Leibniz's Law: for any thing(s) α and β, $\alpha = \beta$ if and only if α and β have all the same properties.

This says that anything(s) that are identical must have the same properties. So, if something(s) α and β have different properties, qualities, or features, then α and β are distinct. For those wanting to argue against CI, if the parts can be shown to have different properties from the whole, then the parts and whole are not identical.

Importantly, the variables 'α' and 'β' in this statement of Leibniz's Law are stand-ins for either plural or singular terms or variables, or a mix of the two. It is a *neutral* statement of Leibniz's Law: it does not specify or presuppose whether the terms we use range over one thing or many. Moreover, the identity predicate used takes either plural or singular terms in its argument places. Classical first-order logic has an identity predicate that allows singular terms, while our plural logic identity predicate allows for plural terms. If we accept CI, then we need to allow for the case when *one* thing is identical to *many*, so that we can express our view and state all of the many–one identity claims that we think are true. Call this *hybrid identity* (Wallace 2011a, 2011b).[52]

One might already be inclined to object to CI on the grounds that it is inexpressible in either first-order classical logic or plural logic. One might insist that the singular or plural identity predicate does not allow for a well-formed statement of the view that one thing is identical to many, so there is no well-formed way to even formulate the CI position.[53] But this is unnecessarily uncharitable. Opponents should at least let the CI theorist use whatever language

---

[51] Some also think that CI entails universalism, or helps provide a permissive answer to SCQ. See, e.g., Merricks (2005), Sider (2007), and Harte (2002). But this is controversial. See, e.g., McDaniel (2010b) and Cameron (2007, 2012).

[52] Bohn (2021) uses a metaphysically neutral, general notion of identity, and a principle of *hybrid indiscernibility of identicals*. Other options are available. What matters for our purposes here is that, however it comes about, both identity and Leibniz's Law can be stated generally, with any combination of either singular or plural terms in the relevant argument places. See Cotnoir (2014b) for discussion.

[53] Cf. Peter van Inwagen's syntactic objections to CI (1994: 211).

she wants to get her view on the table, *then* see whether it can withstand sophisticated scrutiny. Besides, it is easy enough to *add* an identity predicate that allows singular or plural terms in its argument places, as we have done above.

Moreover – and I think that this point is not made often enough in the literature – it is not just the CI theorist who should want to adopt a neutral statement of Leibniz's Law or hybrid identity. Both the nihilist and compositional moderate should want to as well. To see this, let's think like a nihilist for a moment. Consider a world with only three simples. The nihilist thinks that we can quantify over these simples singularly (individually), such as (22):

(22) $\exists x \exists y \exists z (x \neq y \ \& \ y \neq z \ \& \ x \neq z)$

She also thinks that we can quantify over these same simples plurally. So we can quantify over x, y, and z, taken together (call this W), or x and y together (call this U), and so on. We can also state the relevant plural nonidentity claim, such as (23):

(23) $\exists W \exists U (W \neq U)$

Yet the nihilist also thinks that none of the simples taken individually are identical to any of the simples taken plurally. If we have two simples x and y, where $x \neq y$, the nihilist does *not* think that either of these simples taken individually is identical to the simples taken together. If we are new to nihilism and haven't heard of the view, making this clarification may be important in defining her view. We need to know what the view is committed to and what it is not. So she should endorse (24):

(24) $\exists x \exists y \exists U (x \neq U \ \& \ y \neq U)$

However, depending on the plural logic and language that the nihilist accepts, (24) may not be a statement she can express, since it makes use of a hybrid identity predicate. In order to state some of the facts of a nihilist world – i.e., that some of the simples taken individually are *not* identical to some other simples taken collectively, or some other single simple – we need to be able use an identity predicate that allows a combination of plural and singular terms. There may not be any hybrid identity claims that the nihilist thinks are *true*, but there are certainly ones that she thinks are false. And it is important that such claims are registered as legitimately false and not merely nonsensical because the claim under consideration is not well formed in the nihilist's language. The nihilist should be able to express and accept (24), so she should accept a hybrid identity predicate. This point applies, *mutandis mutandis*, to the compositional moderate, whose worldview also includes a variety of (relevant) many–one identity claims that she thinks are false, not merely nonsensical.

3.3 Objections to CI

Arguments against CI tend to fall into two camps: those that do not accept or pay attention to plural logic and, consequently, do not accept or pay attention to the distinction between collective and distributive predicates, and those that do. Let's take the first kind first.

3.3.1 Invalid and Unsound

Here are some common arguments against CI, some of which we mentioned above. The parts are small; the whole is big. The parts are light; the whole is heavy. We can hold the parts in our hand; we cannot hold the whole in our hands. The parts can be next to each other; the whole cannot. And so on. All of these arguments aim to show that there is a property or features that the parts have that the whole does not. By Leibniz's Law, the parts are not identical to the whole.

Yet each of these arguments is provably invalid, if we assume that the premises are true. When we claim that the parts are small, we mean that each part, individually, is small. When we claim that the parts are light, we mean that each part, individually, is light. We can hold some of the parts, individually, in our hand. Some of the parts, individually, can be next to each other. In each case, we are appealing to a property or features that the parts have *distributively*, not collectively. In fact, the logical form of a statement such as "the parts, individually, are small" is different from "the parts, collectively, are small." In the first case, we singularly existentially quantify over each part and predicate of each that it is small; in the second, we plurally existentially quantify over the parts collectively and predicate of them *together* that they are small. Importantly, this second claim is false. The parts taken collectively are *not* small; the parts taken together are exactly as big as the whole!

The CI theorist does not claim that *each* part is identical to the whole. Her claim is that the parts, collectively, are identical to the whole. So if someone wants to appeal to Leibniz's Law to show that the parts have a property that the whole does not, they have to show that the parts *collectively* have a feature that the whole does not. The above (quick) arguments do not do this, rendering them invalid. They syntactically equivocate on how the relevant predicates are applied to the parts, collectively or distributively. Yet if the equivocation is fixed, making the arguments valid, they are then unsound. The parts, collectively, are not small nor light, nor do they fit in our hand, nor are they next to each other. So, there is no violation of Leibniz's Law. So, these arguments can be easily dismissed (Wallace 2011a, 2011b).

3.3.2 Persistence Worries

Not so easily dismissed are the other class of objections against CI. These *do* take into account the distinction between collective and distributive predicates. They are worth taking more seriously. We will divide these up into two camps: *persistence worries* and *numerical worries*. Persistence worries aim to show that the parts have a temporal or modal property that the whole does not have (or the other way around). Numerical worries aim to show that there is something about the *number* of parts and wholes, or how we *count* them, or how we understand something being *one* of some others, that leads to problems for CI. Let's start with the persistence worries.

Temporal Argument. Suppose we have a table composed of numerous molecules. The molecules existed before the table – scattered but existing at some time in the past. Soon, the table will gradually have some parts replaced. It will live a long life, lose some parts, gain some new ones, get refurbished and will eventually be put in a museum because of its historical importance. Meanwhile, the molecules will slowly fall away and eventually stop existing. At a certain point, the table will exist but the molecules will not. Here are some things that are true of the table (whole) and the molecules (parts): the molecules, collectively, existed before the table, yet the table did not exist before the table; the table will exist after the molecules disappear, yet the molecules will not exist after the molecules disappear. In short, the molecules and table have different temporal properties. By Leibniz's Law, the molecules and table are not identical. This point generalizes to any parts and whole. So: composition is not identity.

Modal Argument. Suppose there is a table composed of numerous molecules. The molecules and table have always existed together, and always will. They were created together and will be destroyed together. They share all of their temporal properties. Nonetheless, the table *could have* lost some molecules and survived; the molecules *could not* have lost some of themselves and survived. The molecules *could have* been scattered and survived; the table *could not* have been scattered and survived. In short, the molecules (parts) and table (whole) have different modal properties.[54] By Leibniz's Law, the molecules and table are not identical. This point generalizes to any parts and whole. So: composition is not identity.

---

[54] This argument is a version of Gibbard's (1975) Goliath and Lumpl example, only with a composite object (a table and numerous molecules) instead of a constituted object (a statue and a lump of clay). See, e.g., Wasserman (2021) and Sattig (2021) for a nice overview and discussion.

In response to these persistence worries, the CI theorist has some options. The most promising moves (to my mind) involve the CI theorist taking on some metaphysical commitments about what it is for an object to have temporal or modal properties. In particular, depending on our metaphysical views about how it is that an object instantiates these kinds of features, the CI theorist may insist that the scenarios above are underdescribed, misdescribed, or make some implicit assumptions that she does not accept.

For example, in response to the temporal argument, a lot will depend on her metaphysical view of how objects persist through time. She may claim that the above argument assumes that the table, or molecules, is/are wholly present at every moment that it (they) exists. This is an *endurantist* assumption that she may not accept. Indeed, the temporal argument is crucially an argument about change over time, which – as many philosophical puzzles about change over time show – is generally perplexing *independent* of our view of composition. So the CI theorist's response to the temporal argument may be to embrace a particular metaphysics of time, objects in time, or change over time, which would *supplement* her commitment to CI.

One option is to accept temporal parts and four dimensionalism, and claim that objects are *temporally* extended.[55] An object has temporal properties by being a temporally extended whole with various temporal parts. It is in virtue of these temporal parts having certain properties that the temporally extended whole has temporal properties. In the temporal argument, it was not assumed that the molecules and table were temporally extended objects. If it had been, then we would have an easy answer for why the molecules are not identical to the table – *they have distinct temporal parts*. Compare the temporally extended mereological sum of all of the spatial and temporal parts of the molecules – call this the *transtemporal molecules* (TM) – with the temporally extended mereological sum of all of the spatial and temporal parts of the table – call this the *transtemporal-table* (TT). Then we can see that TM has temporal parts that TT lacks, and TT has temporal parts that TM lacks. So, TM is not identical to TT. But this should be expected! The relevant transtemporal sums only *partially* overlap. It is only in cases where the parts *completely* overlap the whole that we will have a seeming violation of Leibniz's Law. The example in temporal argument is not an instance of complete overlap, so it is not a counterexample to CI.

In response to the modal argument, a lot will depend on the CI theorist's metaphysical view of how objects instantiate modal properties. In the modal argument, we used an example which stipulates that the molecules and the table have all of the same temporal properties. One reason for this is to curtail any move

---

[55] See, e.g., Lewis (1986) and Sider (1997, 2001).

by appealing to temporal parts, or by otherwise showing that the relevant objects are not completely spatio-temporally overlapping. However, the CI theorist has options.

Parallel to the temporal parts move, the CI theorist could embrace *modal parts*. While much more controversial and far less common than temporal parts, a commitment to modal parts is the claim that ordinary objects are *modally* extended.[56] It is the modal analog of temporal parts.

One straightforward way to do this is to assume modal realism. Modal realism is a view about modality that anchors the truth of our modal claims by the activities of individuals in other, concrete possible worlds. Things are possible for individuals in the actual world by the activities of *counterparts* in other possible worlds (Lewis 1986). Alter this view so that individuals are not world bound, but mereological sums *across* worlds, with one part in the actual world, and many other parts (what otherwise would be counterparts) in other worlds. Such *transworld* objects have their modal properties by being extended across possible worlds – mereological sums of world parts. What happens to these world parts grounds the modal facts of the modally extended object.

Go back to the table and its molecules. Compare the modally extended molecules – call this the *transworld molecules* (WM) – with the modally extended table – call this the *transworld table* (WT). Then we can see that WM has modal parts that WT lacks, and WT has modal parts that WM lacks. So, WM is not identical to WT. Importantly, the relevant modally extended sums only *partially* overlap, in the actual world, and maybe in some others; in other worlds, they do not. Yet, assuming CI, it is only in cases where the parts of something *completely* overlap the whole that we will have a seeming violation of Leibniz's Law. If a CI theorist accepts modal parts, then the example in the modal argument is not an instance of complete overlap, so it is not a counterexample to CI.

I mention temporal and modal parts as mere options for the CI theorist. They are not the only available moves (even though they are ones I favor).[57] The broader point is that appealing to temporal or modal properties to object to CI invites turning the conversation toward complicated metaphysical issues about *how* objects have the temporal and modal features that they do. These are tricky and perplexing subjects independent of our views on composition. As such, the

---

[56] For defenders or discussion, see Schlesinger (1985), Hale (1991), Benovsky (2006a, 2006b, 2006c), Cresswell (2010), Yagisawa (2010), Rini and Cresswell (2012), Wallace (2011b, 2014a, 2014b, 2019), Graham (2015), De (2018), Cotnoir and Varzi (2021).

[57] For example, instead of embracing modal parts in the way suggested (as a modal counterpart of temporal worm theory), one could accept modal realism and counterpart theory. See Lewis (1986) and Sider (2001) in response to Gibbard-like colocation worries.

CI theorist's response to temporal and modal arguments may be to embrace a particular metaphysics of time or modality, which would *supplement* her commitment to CI.

Let me put this last point another way. Accepting CI does not tell us which objects exist and what the world is like. It is not a theory of everything. The only explicit commitment that CI makes is a claim about the composition relation – namely, that composition is identity. Otherwise, the view itself is metaphysically neutral. Like mereology, it is consistent with a range of ways the world could be. So it should be somewhat expected that, when faced with an objection such as the temporal or modal argument – arguments that make assumptions about what the world is like or how objects behave – the CI theorist will need to bolster her account with additional metaphysical commitments. Fortunately, CI is consistent with several options, two of which I've mentioned.

3.3.3 Numerical Worries

Let's take a look at the numerical worries. Lewis (1991: 87) articulates one kind of numerical worry as follows: "What's true of the many is not exactly what's true of the one. After all they are many while it is one."

This is an appeal to Leibniz's Law, like the invalid arguments above. Yet importantly this one is valid: the parts collectively are many, while the whole is one. So there is no unwarranted slip here between collective and distributive readings. Call this *the cardinality objection*.

Related to the cardinality objection is the *counting argument*. Take our world with only a coffee mug and a running shoe. A universalist claims that in addition to the mug and shoe, there is also the mereological sum of the mug and shoe, *mugshoe*. Clearly, mugshoe is not identical to the mug, for mugshoe has a part that is a shoe and the mug does not. Nor is mugshoe identical to the shoe, for mugshoe has a part that is a mug and the shoe does not. Given our assumption *count* in the odd universe argument, wholes are distinct from their parts. So, composition is not identity.

The counting argument may seem to make the same mistake as some of the invalid arguments we saw a moment ago. Accepting CI does not commit one to the claim that the whole is identical to the parts, individually, so we shouldn't expect that we will get a distributive identity claim from each part to the whole, as the counting argument seems to assume. But the point is rather this: *given* the way that we count – via singular existential quantifiers and nonidentity claims – when we count up the parts and count up the whole, we will always get *more* things than the number of parts. If we get more things than the number of parts whenever we account for the whole, then the whole must be something in addition to the parts. Hence, composition is not identity.[58]

A third numerical worry has to do with the interplay between our inclusion relation *is one of*, Leibniz's Law, and CI. Suppose we have a thing x and a thing y. We can refer to these things collectively as U. Let's also suppose that U compose z. Because everything is one of itself, z is one of z, but z is not one of U – for U is x and y, taken together. So, by Leibniz's Law, z is *not* identical to U. But, by CI, z *is* identical to U. This is *the argument from is-one-of*.[59]

In response to all three of these numerical worries, the best option (in my mind) is to rethink how we attribute numerical predicates to things, which will require us to reject our traditional (singular) way of counting. It should be noted that while the CI theorist is particularly motivated to reconsider how we count (it will address a slew of objections all at once), I hope it becomes clear from the following discussion that we have plenty of other reasons to rethink our methods of counting, independent of our views on composition.

3.4 Counting

Let's take a closer look at how we usually count, using singular existential quantifiers and singular identity and nonidentity claims. Then we'll introduce a framework for an alternative suggestion.

3.4.1 Singular

According to classical logic, here is how we count up objects in our domain. We get a list of all the things that we existentially quantify over, together with the relevant identity and nonidentity statements. But because it is usually assumed that we employ the singular existential quantifier to say what there is, call this *singular counting*.

Go back to our world with the mug and the shoe, and the mereological sum of them, mugshoe. Neither the mug, the shoe, nor mugshoe are identical. We could express this in classical predicate logic with our earlier sentence, (22):

(22) $\exists x \exists y \exists z (x \neq y \ \& \ x \neq z \ \& \ y \neq z)$

Given how we usually quantify over objects in the world – i.e., with a *singular* existential quantifier—there will be no way to quantify over mereological sums without *adding* to the number of things in our ontology. If the whole just *is* the

---

[58] Payton (2022b) calls this the "Many-More Argument."

[59] Given in Lewis (1991: 87), Yi (1999), Sider (2007, 2014). For more on the exploration of various kinds of CAI with the technical features of plural logic and mereology, see, e.g., Cotnoir (2013), Calosi (2016, 2018), Loss (2018, 2021a, 2021b), and Payton (2021b).

parts, then our counts should bottom out at the level of parts. But it doesn't. So, a commitment to wholes is an additional commitment to parts, in a very literal sense of the word *additional*: it is one more item in our domain. Thus, composition is *not* ontologically innocent, and it *certainly* is not identity (van Inwagen 1994: 213). This (again) is *the counting argument* against CI.

As persuasive as this counting argument may seem, it is woefully uncharitable to any view that takes seriously the claim that there are many–one identities. In particular, it is blatantly question begging against the thesis that composition is identity. As we well know by now, the CI theorist won't claim that the parts *individually* are identical to the whole. She doesn't think, for example, that the mug is identical to mugshoe, nor that the shoe is identical to mugshoe. Rather, she thinks that the mug and the shoe *taken together* are identical to mugshoe. Yet this claim is not even *in* (22). Nor is it in the counting argument.

To be clear, the CI theorist doesn't *reject* (22). In fact, she thinks that (22) is true! But she doesn't think that (22) adequately captures all of the relevant facts about mug and shoe, and she doesn't think that it captures all of the facts about how many things there are. In particular, it is silent on the one crucial identity claim that the CI theorist accepts – namely, that mug and shoe are identical to mugshoe. *This* crucial identity claim – the one that defines her view – does not appear in the objection at all. How could it? Any argument against CI that relies on singular counting will be unable to express the claims that the CI theorist accepts, for the logic employed by singular counting doesn't have the expressive power required to articulate the CI position. Clearly, the CI theorist needs to reject singular counting. Yet how else do we count?

3.4.2 Relative

One option is to accept *relative counting*. According to relative counting, counts of things must be taken relative to a concept or kind. Such a view is suggested by Frege in *The Foundations of Arithmetic*:

> The Iliad, for example, can be thought of as one poem, or as twenty-four Books, or as some large Number of verses; and a pile of cards can be thought of as one pack or as fifty-two cards (§22). *One* pair of boots can be thought of as *two* boots (§25).

In §46, Frege continues,

> It will help to consider number in the context of a judgment that brings out its ordinary use. If, in looking at the same external phenomenon, I can say with equal truth 'This is a copse' and 'These are five trees', or 'Here are four

companies' and 'Here are 500 men', then what changes here is neither the individual nor the whole, the aggregate, but rather my terminology. But that is only the sign of the replacement of one concept by another. This suggests . . . that a statement of number contains an assertion about a concept.

The suggestion here is that we can think of thing(s) in various different ways – e.g., as cards, decks, complete sets of suits, etc. Depending on these various ways of thinking about thing(s), we will have different numbers or counts in answer to, *How many?*

One way to interpret this is to commit to referents having multiple concepts or kinds. So, for example, in the way that 'the evening star' and 'the morning star' are two different descriptions or ways of thinking about a single planet (Venus), so, too, 'fifty-two cards' and 'one deck' are different descriptions or ways of thinking about the things in front of us that we use to play cribbage. No one of these categories is privileged, so there is no nonrelativized answer to the question, *How many things are in front of us?* In short, it is an ill-formed question to ask how many *things* there are, without specifying what kind of things we have in mind. Since this view maintains that one can only take a count *relative* to certain concepts or kinds, call this view *relative counting*.

There is plenty of room for variation here.[60] I consider the following discussion to be a sketch of how we might develop things further on behalf of the CI theorist. What matters for our purposes is that the relative counter is committed to two claims: (i) whenever there are composite objects involved, there is rarely a single numerical answer to the question, *How many things are there?* and (ii) numerical answers should be relativized (either implicitly or explicitly) to a concept or kind. That we sometimes *do* give nonrelativized count statements can be explained by the fact that the concepts or kinds we are interested in are often implicit or pragmatically understood.

Try it. Count the things on your desk. Your answer might be something like: "No problem. There are two coffee mugs, one water bottle, one keyboard, one cat; that's five things!" That wasn't so hard. But you've likely implicitly understood my directive to be something like *count the number of macro things* or *count the number of medium-sized dry goods* or *things you can see without a microscope*. Admittedly, there are lots of molecules and particles on your desk, lots of small scraps of paper or dust that you can barely see, water droplets, water molecules, coffee stains, cat hair, and so on. In practice, then, it seems that we have some concept or kind in mind when we answer nonrelativized counting questions. Thus, *relative counting* is appealing because, on reflection, that's

---

[60] For suggestions, endorsements, and critical discussion, see Wallace (2011a, 2011b), Bohn (2009a, 2011, 2014, 2016, 2021), Spencer (2017), and Payton (2022b).

how it seems we *do* in fact count. (And notice that this appeal holds independently from a commitment to CI.)

How does this help in the case of the numerical worries against CI? Let's take the counting argument first. And let's go back to our world with the mug and the shoe. According to the counting argument against CI, (22) is true:

(22) $\exists x \exists y \exists z (x \neq y \;\&\; x \neq z \;\&\; y \neq z)$

As we pointed out earlier, the CI theorist *accepts* this claim. Ordinarily, we take statements such as (22) to mean "there are three things."[61] But according to CI, this isn't the end of the story: (22) does not exhaust all of the relevant facts about the objects under scrutiny. In particular, it leaves out a crucial many–one identity claim that the CI theorist accepts – namely, that mug (x) and shoe (y) are *collectively* identical to mugshoe (z). This fact *can* be expressed using plural quantifiers and hybrid identity, if we allow ourselves to plurally quantify over mug and shoe collectively by "U" (where U = x and y, collectively):

(25) $\exists x \exists y \exists z \exists U (x \neq y \;\&\; x \neq z \;\&\; y \neq z \;\&\; U = z)$

Importantly, the last conjunct, "U = z," is not a *denial* of (22). Indeed, (22) is a *component* of (25) - and (25) is a claim that the CI theorist understands and accepts as consistent. Sentence (25) merely includes an additional claim, *via* conjunction, crucial for understanding CI.

Put another way, accepting CI is not in any way a denial of any of the quantified singular identity or nonidentity claims that a singular counter accepts. Rather, it is an additional identity claim that the CI theorist insists is compatible with the singular facts. The singular counter resists this claim because our usual way of counting assumes that the CI's plural identity claim is false. Moreover, the singular counter takes sentences like (22) to mean "there are three things." Yet the relative counter denies this. She thinks that there is more to the story about what there is and which identity claims hold. She will not take (22) to mean "there are three things" if there are relevant identity claims that need to be accounted for. And there *are*, if (25) is true.

But then how do we read (25) as far as *counting* goes? It is a nonrelativized statement about what exists, and what things are identical or not identical to other things. The relative counter does not think we can get a count of things without it being relativized to some concept or kind. As such, (25) won't have much use for us in English. A rough gloss would sound something like, "There

---

[61] More carefully, we use statements such as (22) to express "there are at least three things." If we wanted to express that there are exactly or only three things, we would need to add some universal quantifiers and identity claims. Since this complicates things in a way that is not necessary for our purposes, we'll ignore it here.

are two things, and one thing, and the two things taken together are identical to the one thing." Importantly, because the two things taken together are identical to the one thing, we do not double count the two things *and* one thing to get three things. *We do not get the claim that the whole is a third thing from the parts.* Of course, all of this is a bit misleading for the relative counter because she does not think that we can make nonrelativized cardinality ascriptions. So the talk-through in ordinary English is strained. (But notice: it is not impossible. I will come back to this point in Section 3.4.4.)

To fix this, consider the concept or kind *medium-sized dry good* and *scattered object*.[62] A *medium-sized dry good* is a visible macro-object like a breadbox, coffee mug, or running shoe. A scattered object is anything whose parts are significantly spatially separated, such as a scattered deck of cards, a constellation of stars in the sky, a mereological sum with spatially distant parts, etc. Given these concepts, we can ask, *How many medium-sized dry goods are there? How many scattered objects are there?* And the answers seem very clear. There are two medium-sized dry goods (the mug and the shoe). There is one scattered object (mugshoe). If CI is correct, the two medium-sized dry goods are collectively identical to the one scattered object. All three of these claims – especially and including the many–one identity the CI theorist accepts – are legitimate answers to counting questions. And, again: we do not get the conclusion that there are three things.

So in response to the counting objection, the CI theorist rejects singular counting. She insists that the correct way to tally up things in the universe is relative to concepts or kinds. When we count this way, we can account for how it is that wholes are not additional items in our domain. Any parts–whole identity facts will be explicitly stated in our relativized count statements, thereby undermining the counting objection.

In response to the cardinality objection, the strategy is similar. The CI theorist does not think that things can have cardinality properties independent of a way of thinking about them, under a concept or kind. So for any portion of reality – say this stuff right here on my desk that can be thought of 'cards' or 'deck of cards' – the portion of reality itself is not one (full stop) nor fifty-two (full stop). It has no nonrelativized cardinal properties. However, relative to the kind 'cards,' there are fifty-two things, and relative to the kind 'deck of cards,' there is one. Moreover and importantly, the CI theorist accepts the relativized many–one identity claim 'fifty-two cards is identical to one deck.' The main thrust of the cardinality objection is that this many–one identity violates

---

[62] A more developed account on behalf of the CI theorist is needed as to what counts as a legitimate concept or kind. Clearly 'thing' would not be helpful, but in certain contexts 'big thing' and 'little thing' are just fine. What's offered here is a brief sketch; variations are possible depending on how the details are developed.

Leibniz's Law. But there is only a violation if we assume that cardinality ascriptions are absolute, not relativized. If we accept that something(s) before us can be *one* relative to a certain kind and *many* relative to another, there is no contradiction, and no violation of Leibniz's Law.

As for the argument from is-one-of, the argument itself relies on an inclusion predicate that *includes* a cardinality ascription. If a CI theorist accepts relative counting, she will require that the inclusion predicate 'is one of' is relativized on every occasion of use. The example we used to describe the argument did not include concepts or kinds, so let's add them. We'll use *small things* and *big things*. Suppose we have two *small things*, x and y, which we can refer to collectively as U, and one *big thing* z. Suppose that U compose z. Because our counts are relativized, not everything is one of itself, where this count of one is nonrelativized. Yet if we relativize our statements, we get something close: z is one *big thing* of z. But then it is false that z is not one *big thing* of U. In fact, given CI, z is one *big thing* of U, because z is identical to U. Hence, there is no violation of Leibniz's Law, and no contradiction.

In short, a CI theorist will not willingly accept a method of counting that cannot even express the many–one identity claims she endorses. Moreover, relative counting already has a palpable, intuitive appeal, independent of our views of composition. Yet in accepting relative counting, the CI theorist can address all three numerical worries all at once.

Returning to the odd universe argument, nearly all of the reasons that were initially given to support *not-CI* can be shown to be undermined. And while the above discussion is only a gesture at some options for the CI theorist – and while there is much more to say in fleshing out the details of these gestures and the many things that can be said in response to them – it should be clear that CI is not obviously false (as is often assumed in the literature). Yet thinking that CI is obviously false is one of the primary reasons to embrace *not-CI* in the odd universe argument. Without this, the argument is unsound.

3.4.3 Count

I've argued that if we embrace CI, we should reject singular counting and adopt relative counting instead. Does this entail a rejection of *count* as well?

COUNT: we count by listing what there is together with the relevant (non) identity claims.

Fortunately, no. At the start of this Element, it was likely *assumed* that the only way to satisfy *count* is by using singular existential quantifiers and singular identity claims. It was also likely assumed that we can only list how many things there are, nonrelativized. Yet *count*, as stated, doesn't distinguish between singular and plural existence or identity claims. It also doesn't prohibit us from adding concepts or kinds when we list "what there is." A CI theorist who embraces relative counting *agrees* with the claim that we count by listing what there is together with the relevant identity and nonidentity claims. However, she also thinks that there are plural existence claims and singular–plural identity claims that cannot be ignored when we count things up. She also thinks that some of these claims need to be relativized to concepts or kinds. But all of this falls within the bounds of *count*, as stated.

Earlier I had used sentence (25) as an example of the kind of sentence a CI theorist would accept, since it includes the singular existential claims and hybrid identity claims she accepts:

(25) $\exists x \exists y \exists z \exists U(x \neq y \;\&\; x \neq z \;\&\; y \neq z \;\&\; U = z)$

I had said that a rough gloss of this sentence in English would sound something like, "There are two things, and one thing, and the two things are identical to the one thing." I had also said that this talk-through would be strained and misleading for a relative counter. But it is important to see that (25) *can* serve as an answer (however strained or misleading) to how many things there are, even though it is nonrelativized. Suppose we have a world with only two simples, *a* and *b*, and the mereological sum of *a* and *b*, *c*. Sentence (25) accurately represents this world, according to the CI theorist. If we then say, "Ok, sure, but how many things are there?", the CI theorist could use the nonrelativized, awkward read-out of (25) and say, "Well, there are two things and one thing and the two things are identical to the one thing." Or she could give the relativized version: "there are two simples and one mereological sum and the two simples are identical to the one mereological sum." The first answer isn't *wrong*; it's just awkward and impractical. We don't get the *incorrect* conclusion that there are three things, for example. The second answer does a much better job of describing the numerical facts. Yet in both cases, we have counted by saying what there is together with the relevant (non)identity claims. In this way, someone who embraces relative counting can fully accept *count*. She will just deny that accepting *count* entails that we accept singular counting.

Conclusion

A common reaction to metaphysical puzzles such as the odd universe argument is to think that some sort of trick is being played. Some might even insist that, in either the setup or the pursuit, we've fallen prey to trivial matters, elementary confusions, mere wordplay, or ridiculous riddles.[63] Yet one of the benefits of thinking through the odd universe argument is that it crucially relies upon our feeling that there is something ridiculous about it. We see the argument and, for many of us, our first response is: *something has gone weirdly wrong*. Then we're motivated to investigate where things have gone weird or wrong, and – ta da! – we're off doing metaphysics, trying to figure out which of the four assumptions is false.

My own thoughts about how best to solve the problem should now be clear: we should accept *simples*, *unrestricted universalism*, and *count*, with an understanding that count does not entail singular counting. We should also accept CI (reject *composition is not identity*), rendering the argument unsound. One of my reasons for walking through this solution, aside from thinking that it is the most promising, is that it has given us an opportunity to promote two views that are often considered unintuitive or implausible: universalism and CI. While I don't expect to have convinced anyone that either of these views are true, I do hope that I have at least weakened some of the usual resolve against them.

It should be noted that rejecting one (or more) of the four assumptions isn't the only available strategy. At various points, I've emphasized that a source of trouble for the odd universe argument is the fact that it is an a priori argument. While the number of objects in the universe (or Kentucky or the sock drawer) may very well be odd, it's the fact that we don't think an a priori argument should be able to prove this sort of fact that strikes many of us as implausible. The general argument is something like, "Well, even if this wacky metaphysical conclusion happens to be true, we can't expect an a priori argument to deliver a conclusion on such matters." Most days, this strikes me as correct, and convincing. Arguments from the armchair can only be so powerful. Nonetheless, if we philosophers aren't allowed to occasionally appeal to a priori arguments for metaphysically robust conclusions, what else should we expect ourselves to be doing? If philosophy is in the business of figuring out what the world is like through analysis, reflection, and argumentation, we should expect to occasionally come to surprising, substantial metaphysical conclusions through a priori reasoning. Perhaps we, like Descartes, *can* prove our own existence just by thinking about it. Or perhaps we can prove that god exists just by contemplating the greatest conceivable thing. Or maybe we can show that there are numbers, or properties, or possible worlds, just by thinking about and reflecting on mathematics and logic. If so, then perhaps it isn't so strange to conclude a priori that there is an odd number of things in the universe. I don't personally think this is right, of course; my preferred response is still to

---

[63] See, e.g., Carnap (1950), Bennett (2009), Hirsch (2011), and Thomasson (2017).

embrace CI. But after having spent so much of this Element mapping out available moves to show where to resist the conclusion, I would be remiss to not mention that it is also an option to embrace it.

However we decide to respond to the odd universe argument, it is clear that thinking through it connects us to a broad range of topics in philosophy – change, persistence, identity, and modality – involving any objects we care to think of. True, this Element primarily uses examples of ordinary (boring) objects such as tables, chairs, coffee mugs, and running shoes. But it is clear that we think of many different kinds of things in terms of parts and wholes, as our sentences 1–16 at the beginning of our discussion illustrate. All of our conclusions concerning coffee mugs and running shoes apply *mutatis mutandis* to these other things, too. What's more, we often appeal to the language of parts and wholes when thinking about those things that are most important to us. People we love are part of us. Loved ones make us whole. When we suffer loss, part of us is missing. Momentous occasions build integral parts of our character. Our values are a crucial part of who we are. A community makes many individuals one. Perhaps, you think, this is just a way of talking, a figure of speech. Even so, the fact that we appeal to the metaphor of parts and wholes to emphasize the intensity of our sentiments is a testament to our very high opinion of mereological imagery. It is quite impressive how often we do this and how natural doing so seems to be. So perhaps even more surprising than the odd universe conclusion is the fact that solving it requires us to reflect on some of the most fundamental ways we understand ourselves and the world. If the odd universe argument is a trick, we must admit: it's a really good one.

References

Armstrong, D. M. (1978) *Universals and Scientific Realism*. Cambridge: Cambridge University Press.

Armstrong, D. M. (1997) *A World of States of Affairs*. Cambridge: Cambridge University Press.

Bagaria, J. (2021) "Set Theory" in Zalta, E. N. (ed.), *The Stanford Encyclopedia of Philosophy* (winter ed.). https://plato.stanford.edu/archives/win2021/entries/set-theory.

Barnes, E. (2007) "Vagueness and Arbitrariness: Merricks on Composition" *Mind* 116(461): 105–113.

Baxter, D. (1988a) "Many-One Identity" *Philosophical Papers* 17(3): 193–216.

Baxter, D. (1988b) "Identity in the Loose and Popular Sense" *Mind* 97(388): 575–582.

Baxter, D. (2014) "Identity, Discernibility, and Composition" in Cotnoir, A., and Baxter, D. (eds.), *Composition as Identity*. Oxford: Oxford University Press, 244–253.

Bennett, K. (2009) "Composition, Colocation, and Metaontology" in Chalmers, D. J., Manley, R., and Wasserman R. (eds.), *Metametaphysics: New Essays on the Foundations of Ontology*. Oxford: Oxford University Press, 38–76.

Bennett, K. (2015) "Perfectly Understood, Unproblematic, and Certain: Lewis on Mereology" in Loewer, B., and Schaffer, J. (eds.), *A Companion to David Lewis*. Chichester, UK: Wiley-Blackwell, 250–261.

Benovsky, J. (2006a) "A Modal Bundle Theory" *Metaphysica* 7: 21–33.

Benovsky, J. (2006b) "Four-Dimensionalism and Modal Perdurants" in Valore, P. (ed.), *Topics on General and Formal Ontology*. Milan, Italy: Polimetrica, 137–159.

Benovsky, J. (2006c) *Persistence through Time and across Possible Worlds*. Frankfurt: Ontos Verlag.

Bohn, E. (2009a) "An Argument against the Necessity of Unrestricted Composition" *Analysis* 69(1): 27–31.

Bohn, E. (2009b) "Must There Be a Top Level?" *Philosophical Quarterly* 59 (235): 193–201.

Bohn, E. (2011) "Commentary on 'Parts of Classes'" *Humana. Mente* 19: 151–158.

Bohn, E. (2014) "Unrestricted Composition as Identity" in Cotnoir, A., and Baxter, D. (eds.), *Composition as Identity*. Oxford: Oxford University Press, 143–165.

Bohn, E. (2016) "Composition as Identity and Plural Cantor's Theorem" in *Logic and Logical Philosophy* 25(3): 411–428.

Bohn, E. (2021) "Composition as Identity: Pushing Forward" *Synthese* 198 (Suppl. 18): 4595–4607.

Boolos, G. (1984) "To Be Is to Be a Value of a Variable (or to Be Some Values of Some Variables)" *Journal of Philosophy* 81(8): 430–450. Reprinted in Boolos, G. (1998) Logic, Logic, and Logic. Cambridge, MA: Harvard University Press.

Boolos, G. (1985) "Nominalist Platonism" *Philosophical Review* 94(3): 327–344. Reprinted in Boolos, G. (1998) Logic, Logic, and Logic. Cambridge, MA: Harvard University Press.

Bricker, P. (2016) "Composition as a Kind of Identity" *Inquiry: An Interdisciplinary Journal of Philosophy* 59(3): 264–294.

Bricker, P. (2019) "Composition as Identity, Leibniz's Law, and Slice-Sensitive Emergent Properties" *Synthese* 198: 4389–4409.

Brzozowski, J. (2016) "Monism and Gunk" in Jago, M. (ed.), *Reality Making*. Oxford: Oxford University Press, 57–74.

Burgess, J. (2022) *Set Theory*, Elements in Philosophy and Logic. Cambridge: Cambridge University Press.

Calosi, C. (2016) "Composition as Identity and Mereological Nihilism" *Philosophical Quarterly* 66(263): 219–235.

Calosi, C. (2018) "Failure or Boredom: The Pendulum of Composition as Identity" *American Philosophical Quarterly* 55(3): 281–292.

Calosi, C. (2021) "Is Parthood Identity?" *Synthese* 198: 4503–4517.

Cameron, R. (2007) "The Contingency of Composition" *Philosophical Studies* 136(1): 99–121.

Cameron, R. (2012) "Composition as Identity Does Not Settle the Special Composition Question" *Philosophy and Phenomenological Research* 84(3): 531–554.

Cameron, R. (2014) "Parts Generate the Whole but They Are Not Identical to It" in Cotnoir, A., and Baxter, D., *Composition as Identity*. Oxford: Oxford University Press, 90–107.

Carnap, R. (1950) "Empiricism, Semantics, and Ontology" *Revue Internationale de Philosophie* 4: 20–40.

Casati, R., and Varzi, A. C. (1999) *Parts and Places: The Structures of Spatial Representation*. Cambridge, MA: MIT Press.

Casati, R., and Varzi, A. (2008) *Insurmountable Simplicities: Thirty-Nine Philosophical Conundrums*. New York: Columbia University Press.

Chalmers, D. J., Manley, R., and Wasserman, R. (eds.) (2009) *Metametaphysics: New Essays on the Foundations of Ontology*. Oxford: Oxford University Press.

Cotnoir, A. (2013) "Composition as General Identity" in Bennett, K., and Zimmerman, D. (eds.), *Oxford Studies in Metaphysics*, vol. 8. Oxford: Oxford University Press, 295–322.

Cotnoir, A. (2014a) "Universalism and Junk" *Australasian Journal of Philosophy* 4(92): 649–664.

Cotnoir, A. (2014b) "Composition as Identity: Framing the Debate" in Cotnoir, A., and Baxter, D. (eds.), *Composition as Identity*. Oxford: Oxford University Press, 3–23.

Cotnoir, A., and Baxter, D. (2014) *Composition as Identity*. Oxford: Oxford University Press.

Cotnoir, A., and Varzi, A. (2021) *Mereology*. Oxford: Oxford University Press.

Cowling, S. (2014) "No Simples, No Gunk, No Nothing" *Pacific Philosophical Quarterly* 95(1): 246–260.

Cresswell, M. J. (2010) "Predicate Wormism: A Quinean Account of De Re Modality" *Logique et Analyse* 53(212): 449–464.

Dasgupta, S. (2009) "Individuals: An Essay in Revisionary Metaphysics" *Philosophical Studies* 145: 35–67.

De, M. (2018) "On the Humphrey Objection to Modal Realism" *Grazer Philosopische Studien* 95:159–179.

Dorr, C., and Rosen, G. (2002) "Composition as a Fiction" in Gale, R. (ed.), *The Blackwell Guide to Metaphysics*. Oxford: Blackwell, 151–174.

Effingham, N. (2011) "Sider, Hawley, Sider and the Vagueness Argument" *Philosophical Studies* 154: 241–250.

Fairchild, M., and Hawthorne, J. (2018) "Against Conservativism in Metaphysics" *Royal Institute of Philosophy Supplements* 82: 45–75.

Fairchild, M. (2021) "Arbitrariness and the Long Road to Permissivism" *Noûs* 56(3): 619–638. https://doi.org/10.1111/nous.12376.

Gibbard, A. (1975) "Contingent Identity" *Journal of Philosophical Logic* 4: 187–221.

Goodman, N. (1951) *The Structure of Appearances*. Cambridge, MA: Harvard University Press.

Goodman, N. (1977) *The Structure of Appearances*. Cambridge, MA: Harvard University Press.

Graham, A. (2015) "From Four- to Five-Dimenionalism" *Ratio* 28(1): 14–18.

Hale, S. (1991) "Modal Realism without Counterparts" *Southwest Philosophy Review* 7: 77–86.

Harte, V. (2002) *Plato on Parts and Wholes: The Metaphysics of Structure*. Oxford: Oxford University Press.

Hawley, K. (2014) "Ontological Innocence" in Cotnoir, A., and Baxter, D. (eds), *Composition as Identity*. Oxford: Oxford University Press: 70–89.

Hirsch, E. (2011) *Quantifier Variance and Realism: Essays in Metaontology*. New York: Oxford University Press.

Hofweber, T. (2009) "Ambitious, yet Modest, Metaphysics" in Chalmers, D. J., Manley, R., and Wasserman, R. (eds.), *Metametaphysics: New Essays on the Foundations of Ontology.* Oxford: Oxford University Press, 260–289.

Hovda, P. (2009) "What Is Classical Mereology?" *Journal of Philosophical Logic* 38: 55–82.

Hudson, H. (2007) "Simples and Gunk," *Philosophy Compass* 2: 291–302.

Huggett, N. (2019) "Zeno's Paradoxes" in Zalta, E. N. (ed.), *The Stanford Encyclopedia of Philosophy* (winter ed.). https://plato.stanford.edu/arch ives/win2019/entries/paradox-zeno/.

Hyde, D., and Raffman, D. (2018) "Sorites Paradox" in Zalta, E. N. (ed.), *The Stanford Encyclopedia of Philosophy* (summer ed.). https://plato.stanford .edu/archives/sum2018/entries/sorites-paradox/.

Kleinschmidt, S. (ed.) (2014) *Mereology and Location.* New York: Oxford University Press.

Kleinschmidt, S. (2019) "Fusion First" *Nous* 53(3): 689–707.

Korman, D. (2015) *Objects: Nothing Out of the Ordinary.* Oxford: Oxford University Press.

Korman, D. (2020a) "Conservatism, Counterexamples, and Debunking" *Analysis* 80(3): 558–574.

Korman, D. (2020b) "Ordinary Objects" in Zalta, E. N. (ed.), The Stanford Encyclopedia of Philosophy (fall ed.). https://plato.stanford.edu/archives/ fall2020/entries/ordinary-objects/.

Lando, G. (2017) *Mereology: A Philosophical Introduction.* London: Bloomsbury Academic.

Leonard, H. S., and Goodman, N. (1940) "The Calculus of Individuals and Its Uses" *Journal of Symbolic Logic* 5(2): 45–55.

Leśniewski, S. (1927–31) "O podstawach matematyki" *Przeglad Filozoficzny* 30: 164–206; 31: 261–291; 32: 60–101; 33: 77–105; 34: 142–170. Translated by V. F. Sinisi as "Leśniewski's Foundations of Mathematics" *Topoi* 2 (1983): 3–52. Translated by D. I. Barnett as "On the Foundations of Mathematics" in S. Leśniewski, *Collected Works*, vol. 1, ed. by S. J. Surma et al. Dordrecht: Kluwer, 1992, 174–382.

Lewis, D. (1986) *On the Plurality of Worlds.* Malden, MA: Blackwell.

Lewis, D. (1991) *Parts of Classes.* Cambridge, MA: Blackwell.

Lewis, D. (1994) "Reduction of Mind" in Guttenplan, S. (ed.), *Companion to the Philosophy of Mind.* Oxford: Blackwell, 412–431.

Linnebo, Ø. (2022) "Plural Quantification" in Zalta, E. N. (ed.), The Stanford Encyclopedia of Philosophy (spring ed.). https://plato.stanford.edu/archives/ spr2022/entries/plural-quant/.

Loss, R. (2018) "A Sudden Collapse to Nihilism" *Philosophical Quarterly* 68 (271): 370–375.

Loss, R. (2021a) "Composition, Identity, and Plural Ontology" *Synthese* 198: 9193–9210.

Loss, R. (2021b) "On Atomic Composition as Identity" *Synthese* 198 (Suppl. 18): 4519–4542.

Loss, R. (2022) "Composition as Identity and the Innocence of Mereology" *Philosophy and Phenomenological Research* 105: 128–143.

Lycan, W. (2001) "Moore against the New Sceptics" *Philosophical Studies* 103: 35–53.

Lycan, W. (2019) *On Evidence in Philosophy*. Oxford: Oxford University Press.

Markosian, N. (2005) "Against Ontological Fundamentalism" *Facta Philosophica* 7: 69–83.

Markosian, N. (2015) "The Right Stuff" *Australasian Journal of Philosophy* 93: 665-668.

McDaniel, K. (2010a) "Parts and Wholes" *Philosophy Compass*: 412–425.

McDaniel, K. (2010b) "Composition as identity Does Not Entail Universalism" *Erkenntnis* 73(1): 97–100.

McDaniel, K. (2014) "Parthood Is Identity" in Kleinshmidt, S. (ed.), *Mereology and Location*. New York: Oxford University Press.

McKay, T. (2006) *Plural Predication*. Oxford: Oxford University Press.

Mellor, D. H. (2006) "Wholes and Parts: The Limits of Composition" *South African Journal of Philosophy* 25(2): 138–145.

Merricks, T. (1999) "Composition as Identity, Mereological Essentialism, and Counterpart Theory" *Australasian Journal of Philosophy* 77: 192–195.

Merricks, T. (2001) *Objects and Persons*. Oxford: Clarendon Press.

Merricks, T. (2005) "Composition and Vagueness" *Mind* 114(455): 615–637.

Moore, G. E. (1959) "Proof of an External World" in Moore, G. E. (ed.), *Philosophical Papers*. London: Allen and Unwin, 144–148.

Oliver, A., and Smiley, T. (2016) *Plural Logic*. 2nd ed. Oxford: Oxford University Press.

Parsons, J. (2014) "The Many Primitives of Mereology" in Kleinschmidt, S. (ed.), *Mereology and Location*. New York: Oxford University Press.

Payton, J. (2021a) "How to Identify Wholes with Their Parts" *Synthese* 198 (Suppl. 18): 4571–4593.

Payton, J. (2021b) "Composition as Identity, Now with All the Pluralities You Could Want" *Synthese* 199: 8047–8068.

Payton, J. (2022a) "Composition and Plethological Innocence" *Analysis* 82(1): 67–74.

Payton, J. (2022b) "Counting Composites" *Australasian Journal of Philosophy* 100(4): 695–710.

Quine, W. V. O. (1948) "On What There Is" *Review of Metaphysics* 2: 21–38.

Rini, A. A., and Cresswell, M. J. (2012) *The World-Time Parallel: Tense and Modality in Logic and Metaphysics*. Cambridge: Cambridge University Press.

Sainsbury, R. M. (2009) *Paradoxes*. 3rd ed. Cambridge: Cambridge University Press.

Salmon, W. C. (ed.) (2001) *Zeno's Paradoxes*. Indianapolis, IN: Hackett Publishing Inc.

Sattig, T. (2021) *Material Objects*, Elements in Metaphysics. Cambridge: Cambridge University Press.

Schaffer, J. (2010) "Monism: The Priority of the Whole" *Philosophical Review* 119: 31–76.

Schlesinger, G. N. (1985) "Spatial, Temporal, and Cosmic Parts" *Southern Journal of Philosophy*, 23: 255–271.

Shapiro, S., and Kissel, T. (2022) *Classical First-Order Logic*, Elements in Philosophy and Logic. Cambridge: Cambridge University Press.

Sider, T. (1993) "Van Inwagen and the Possibility of Gunk" *Analysis* 53: 285–289.

Sider, T. (1997) "Four-Dimensionalism" *Philosophical Review* 106: 197–231.

Sider, T. (2001) *Four-Dimensionalism*. Oxford: Oxford University Press.

Sider, T. (2007) "Parthood" *Philosophical Review* 116: 51–91.

Sider, T. (2011) *Writing the Book of the World*. Oxford: Oxford University Press.

Sider, T. (2013) "Against Parthood" in Bennett, K., and Zimmerman, D. (eds.), *Oxford Studies in Metaphysics*, vol. 8. Oxford: Oxford University Press, 237–293.

Sider, T. (2014) "Consequences of Collapse" in Cotnoir, A., and Baxter, D. (eds.), *Composition as Identity*. Oxford: Oxford University Press, 211–221.

Simons, P. (1987) *Parts: A Study in Ontology*. Oxford: Oxford University Press.

Sorenson, R. (2003) *A Brief History of the Paradox: Philosophy and the Labyrinths of the Mind*. Oxford: Oxford University Press.

Spencer, J. (2017) "Counting on Strong Composition as Identity to Settle the Special Composition Question" *Erkenntnis* 82(4): 857–872.

Thomasson, A. (2017) "Metaphysical Disputes and Metalinguistic Negotiation" *Analytic Philosophy* 58(1): 1–28.

Turner, J. (2014) "Donald Baxter's Composition as Identity" in Cotnoir, A., and Baxter, D. (eds), *Composition as Identity*. Oxford: Oxford University Press, 225–243.

Unger, P. (1979a) "There Are No Ordinary Things" *Synthese* 41:117–154.

Unger, P. (1979b) "I Do Not Exist" in Macdonald, G. F. (ed.), *Perception and Identity*. Ithaca, NY: Cornell University Press, 235–251.

Uzquiano, G. (2006) "The Price of Universality" *Philosophical Studies* 129: 137–169.

Van Cleve, J. (2008) "The Moon and Sixpence: A Defense of Mereological Universalism" in Sider, T., Hawthorne, J., and Zimmerman D. W. (eds.), *Contemporary Debates in Metaphsyics*. Malden, MA: Blackwell, 321–340.

Van Inwagen, P. (1981) "The Doctrine of Arbitrary Undetached Parts" *Pacific Philosophical Quarterly* 62: 123–137.

Van Inwagen, P. (1987) "When Are Objects Parts?" *Philosophical Perspectives* 1: 21–47.

Van Inwagen, P. (1990) *Material Beings*. Ithaca, NY: Cornell University Press.

Van Inwagen, P. (1994) "Composition as Identity" *Philosophical Perspectives* 8: 207–220.

Varzi, A. (2014) "Counting and Countenancing" in Cotnoir, A., and Baxter, D. (eds), *Composition as Identity*. Oxford: Oxford University Press, 47–69.

Varzi, A. (2019) "Mereology" in Zalta, E. N. (ed.), *The Stanford Encyclopedia of Philosophy* (spring ed.). https://plato.stanford.edu/archives/spr2019/entries/mereology/.

Wallace, M. (2011a) "Composition as Identity: Part 1" *Philosophy Compass* 6 (11): 804–816.

Wallace, M. (2011b) "Composition as Identity: Part 2" *Philosophy Compass* 6 (11): 817–827.

Wallace, M. (2014a) "Composition as Identity, Modal Parts, and Mereological Essentialism" in Cotnoir, A., and Baxter, D. (eds.), *Composition as Identity*. Oxford: Oxford University Press, 211–221.

Wallace, M. (2014b) "The Argument from Vagueness for Modal Parts" *dialectica* 68(3): 355–373.

Wallace, M. (2019) "The Lump Sum: A Theory of Modal Parts" *Philosophical Papers* 48(3): 403–435.

Wallace, M. (2021) "The Polysemy of 'Part'" *Synthese* 198 (Suppl. 18): 4331–4354.

Wasserman, R. (2021) "Material Constitution" in Zalta, E. N. (ed.), The Stanford Encyclopedia of Philosophy (fall ed.). https://plato.stanford.edu/archives/fall2021/entries/material-constitution/.

Yablo, S. (1987) "Identity, Essence, and Indiscernibility" *Journal of Philosophy* 84(6): 293–314.

Yagisawa, T. (2010) *Worlds and Individuals, Possible and Otherwise*. Oxford: Oxford University Press.

Yi, B.-U. (1999) "Is Mereology Ontologically Innocent?" *Philosophical Studies* 93(2): 141–160.

Yi, B.-U. (2005) "The Logic and Meaning of Plurals. Part 1" *Journal of Philosophical Logic* 34: 459–506.

Yi, B.-U. (2006) "The Logic and Meaning of Plurals. Part 2" *Journal of Philosophical Logic* 35: 239–288.

Acknowledgements

I am grateful to a number of folks who read drafts, gave feedback, or otherwise put up with me as I talked through or thought about things while writing this. First to my partner, Aaron Johnson, for his invaluable comments, love, and support throughout. Many thanks also to Aaron Cotnoir, Daniel Nolan, Ted Sider, and Tim Sundell for reading or listening to portions of this project at various stages, and to a small writing group with Lindsey, Molly, Kevin, and Julia, that importantly got things started. I am particularly thankful for two anonymous referees who gave substantive, careful feedback on a rather messy draft, and to Tuomas Tahko for his patience and work as editor. Finally, thank you to my running partner and colleague, Kayla Bohannon, who understands that philosophy is often best slogged out slowly over miles with a friend, not over pages in isolation.

This Element is lovingly dedicated to Aaron, Oz, Lock, and Zuki – the best and silliest parts of a very good life.

Cambridge Elements ≡

Metaphysics

Tuomas E. Tahko

University of Bristol

Tuomas E. Tahko is Professor of Metaphysics of Science at the University of Bristol, UK. Tahko specializes in contemporary analytic metaphysics, with an emphasis on methodological and epistemic issues: 'meta-metaphysics'. He also works at the interface of metaphysics and philosophy of science: 'metaphysics of science'. Tahko is the author of *Unity of Science* (Cambridge University Press, 2021, *Elements in Philosophy of Science*), *An Introduction to Metametaphysics* (Cambridge University Press, 2015) and editor of *Contemporary Aristotelian Metaphysics* (Cambridge University Press, 2012).

About the series

This highly accessible series of Elements provides brief but comprehensive introductions to the most central topics in metaphysics. Many of the Elements also go into considerable depth, so the series will appeal to both students and academics. Some Elements bridge the gaps between metaphysics, philosophy of science, and epistemology.

Cambridge Elements ☰

Metaphysics

A full series listing is available at: www.cambridge.org/EMPH

Printed in the United States
by Baker & Taylor Publisher Services